WHAT IS PRIDE?
AND
WHAT IS ITS OUTCOME?

DAVID JENSEN

ISBN 978-1-68517-842-0 (paperback)
ISBN 978-1-68517-843-7 (digital)

Christian Faith Publishing
832 Park Avenue
Meadville, PA 16335
www.christianfaithpublishing.com

Printed in the United States of America

Introduction

Pride is one of the sins of man that seems to not be dealt with as much in the church today, especially in the United States. Yet it is the one sin the Lord hates the most. Proverbs 6:16–19 tells us seven things God hates, and pride is at the top of the list.

Pride is what caused one third of the angels to fall with Lucifer, and it is what caused man's fall in the garden when he wanted to be like God and was convinced to eat the fruit of the tree of the knowledge of good and evil.

Pride caused man to become violent, plunging the world into chaos and causing God to destroy it in a great flood.

Pride kept man from dispersing throughout the earth, which was commanded by God. Man built a tower to the heavens because he still wanted to unseat the Lord from his throne. Confusing the languages helped slow man's progress toward war with God, but pride is still in his heart.

Pride would cause nations to war against each other, conquering lands so they can rule over others. Empires such Babylon, Assyria, Persia, Greece, and Rome conquered much land and proud men sought to rule the world.

Today most nations are united through an organization located in New York City called the United Nations. This godless entity is ultimately designed to unite the world and eventually battle against God Almighty Himself.

It is established in the proudest nation on earth, the United States. You can see it in the many flags displayed stating *pride* and the numerous decals applied on the rear of automobiles boasting

American pride. You can see it in the products produced in the United States. *Made with Pride in the USA*, the label will say, emblazoned with the large image of the red, white, and blue flag of the United States.

Many Christian churches across the US are also very proud of the country they are located in. Many apostate denominations have sprung up in the Christian faith. They are obsessed with prosperity and wealth and how they are equal with God, being little gods themselves.

The Bible strictly condemns pride in any form. Every time pride is mentioned in Scripture, it is in a negative light.

The spirit of pride made its way into the United States through secret societies. Zechariah 5:1–11 describes its entrance to the new world in 1776 through Adam Weishaupt. This will be explained later in the book.

The antichrist will establish his rule through the United Nations. The United States will turn against its people, especially those of the Christian faith. They will call it a hate organization for its preaching against sin. But the Lord will deal with that pride to Babylon the Great's demise.

Many will become angry about this teaching and are probably already while reading this introduction. But only the humble heart will understand that all nations are against God and that His people are to come out of them and be separate. We are to tell people to repent from their sin and humble themselves and turn to the Lord Jesus Christ.

If you are offended by this message, then ask yourself, "Am I truly humble before God, or is my pride in country getting in the way?"

It is all right to be involved in the democratic process and in community events, but keep in mind the nation will turn against its people. That is prophesied.

Satan

Let us start with the first one to become full of pride. Lucifer became jealous of the worship of Yahweh. He wanted it for himself. He convinced one third of the angels to try and overthrow the throne of the Most High God.

> How you are fallen from heaven, O Lucifer, son of the morning! How you are cut down to the ground, you who weakened the nations! For you have said in your heart: "I will ascend to heaven, I will exalt my throne above the stars of God; I will also sit on the mount of the congregation on the farthest sides of the north; I will ascend above the heights of the clouds, I will be like the most high." Yet you shall be brought down to sheol, to the lowest depths of the pit. (Isaiah 14:12–15)

> And He said to them, "I saw Satan fall like lightning from heaven." (Luke 10:18)

> And another sign appeared in heaven; behold, a great, fiery red dragon having seven heads and ten horns, and seven diadems on his heads. His tail drew a third of the stars of heaven and threw them to the earth. And war broke out in heaven, Michael and his angels fought with the dragon; and the dragon and his angels fought,

but they did not prevail, nor was a place found for them in heaven any longer. So, the great dragon was cast out, that serpent of old, called the devil and Satan, who deceives the whole world; he was cast to the earth, and his angels were cast out with him. (Revelation 12:3, 4, 7–9)

Satan failed in overthrowing Yahweh from his throne. Yet he still wants that praise, so he has been deceiving people since Adam and Eve in the garden.

The Hebrew word for *Lucifer* is *Heylel* (hay-lale'), the morning star: shine, brightness; hence, to make a show, to boast, and thus to be foolish.

You will see this throughout the study. The children of Satan are like their father.

Satan's Deception

Now the serpent was more cunning than any beast of the field which the Lord God had made, and he said to the woman, "Has God indeed said, 'You shall not eat of every tree of the garden?'" And the woman said to the serpent, "We may eat the fruit of the trees of the garden, but the fruit of the tree, which is in the midst of the garden, God has said, 'You shall not eat it, nor shall you touch it, lest you die.'"

Then the serpent said to the woman, "You will not surely die. For God knows that in the day you eat of it your eyes will be opened, and you will be like God, knowing good and evil."

So, when the woman saw that the tree was good for food, that it was pleasant to the eyes, and a tree desirable to make one wise, she took of its fruit and ate. And also gave to her husband with her, and he ate. Then the eyes of both of them were opened, and they knew that they were naked. And they sewed fig leaves together and made themselves coverings.

And they heard the sound of the Lord God walking in the garden in the cool of the day, and Adam and his wife hid themselves from the presence of the Lord God among the trees of the garden. Then the Lord God called to Adam and said to him, "Where are you?" So, he said, "I heard your voice in the garden, and I was afraid, because I was naked, and I hid myself." And He said, "Who told you that you were naked? Have you eaten from the tree of which I commanded you that you should not eat?"

Then the man said, "The woman whom you gave to be with me, she gave me of the tree, and I ate." And the Lord said to the woman, "What is this you have done?" and the woman said, "The serpent deceived me, and I ate."

So the Lord God said to the serpent, "Because you have done this, you are cursed more than all cattle, and more than every beast of the field. On your belly you shall go, and you shall eat dust all the days of your life. And I will put enmity between you and the woman, and between your seed and her seed; He shall bruise your head, and you shall bruise his heel."

To the woman, he said, "I will greatly multiply your sorrow and your conception, in pain you shall bring forth children, your desire shall be for your husband, and he shall rule over you."

Then to Adam he said, "Because you have heeded the voice of your wife and have eaten from the tree of which I commanded you, saying, 'You shall not eat of it,' cursed is the ground for your sake, in toil you shall eat of it all the days of your life. Both thorns and thistles it shall bring forth for you, and you shall eat the herb of the field, in the sweat of your face you shall eat bread till you return to the ground, for out of it you were taken, for dust you are, and to dust you shall return." (Genesis 3:1–19)

From the beginning, Satan lied to get people to follow him. You see, here he twisted what God had commanded to make this sin look appealing. This ultimately caused mankind to fall from God. Satan was forced to earth, where it is now his kingdom. And it is here he deceived the nations so that they will follow and worship him.

The Tower of Rebellion

From the time of Adam's fall to the days of Noah, the world would become violent. God was disappointed that he created man and was set to destroy him. But Noah found favor in God's sight and God preserved him, his wife, his three sons, and their wives from the flood.

After the flood, they were instructed by God to disperse and fill the earth. Flavius Josephus explains what happened next:

> Now the sons of Noah were three—Shem, Japhet, and Ham, born one hundred years before the deluge. These first of all descended from the mountains into the plains and fixed their habitation there, and persuaded others who were greatly afraid of the lower grounds on account of the flood, and so were very loath to come down from the higher places, to venture to follow their examples.
>
> Now the plain in which they first dwelt was called Shinar. God also commanded them to send colonies abroad, for the thorough peopling of the earth, that they might not raise seditions among themselves but might cultivate a great part of the earth and enjoy its fruits after a plentiful manner: But they were so ill instructed that they did not obey God, for which reason they fell into calamities, and were made sensible, by expe-

rience, of what sin they had been guilty; for when they flourished with a numerous youth, God admonished them again to send out colonies; but they, imagining the prosperity they enjoyed was not derived from the favor of God, but supposing that their own power was the proper cause of the plentiful condition they were in, did not obey Him. Ney, they added to this their disobedience to the divine will, the suspicion that they were therefore ordered to send out separate colonies, that being divided asunder, they might the more easily be oppressed.

Now it was Nimrod who excited them to such an affront and contempt of God. He was the grandson of Ham, the son of Noah—a bold man, and of great strength of hand. He persuaded them not to ascribe to God, as if it was through his means they were happy, but to believe that it was their own courage which procured that happiness. He also gradually changed the government into tyranny, seeing no other way of turning men from the fear of God but bring them into a constant dependence upon his power. He also said he would be revenged on God, if he should have a mind to drown the world again; for that he would avenge himself on God for destroying their forefathers!

Now the multitude were very ready to follow the determination of Nimrod, and to esteem it a piece of cowardice to submit to God; and they built a tower, neither sparing any pains, nor being in any degree negligent about the work; and, by reason of the multitude of hands employed in it, it grew very high, sooner than anyone could expect; but the thickness of it was so great, and it was so strongly built, that thereby its great height seemed, upon the view, to be less than it really was. It was built of burnt brick, cemented together with mortar, made of bitumen, that it might not be liable to admit water. When God saw that they acted so madly, He did not resolve to destroy them utterly, since they were not grown wiser by the destruction of the former sinners; but he caused a tumult among them, by producing in them divers' languages; and causing that, through the multitude of those languages, they should not be able to understand one another. The place wherein they built the tower is now called Babylon; because of the confusion of that language which they readily understood before; for the Hebrews mean by the word babel, confusion. (Josephus book I, chapter IV)

The sibyl also makes mention of this tower, and of the confusion of the language, when she says thus:

When all men were of one language, some of them built a high tower, as if they would thereby ascend up to heaven; but the gods sent storms of wind and overthrew the tower and gave everyone his peculiar language." But as to the plain of Shinar, in the country of Babylonia, Hestiaeus mentions it when he says thus: "Such of the priests as were saved, took the sacred vessels of Jupiter Enyalius, and came to Shinar of Babylonia. (Josephus book 1, chapter IV)

Nimrod, who is the grandson of Ham and great-grandson of Noah, is the thirteenth generation from Adam. (In scripture 13 is a number representing rebellion. In Genesis 14:4, it says, twelve years they served Chedorlaomer, and in the thirteenth year they rebelled.

We also see that Nimrod is the thirteenth generation from Adam, and he caused all to rebel.)

The word used for tower in Scripture is *migdalah,* meaning pyramidal. This word is from the prim root word *gadal.* It means to make large as in body, mind, estate, or honor, also in pride, to boast, magnify.

Not only was this a huge structure, but this was total pride and arrogance. After the flood, man was instructed to disperse over the whole earth. Instead, they came together as a united people to build a tower in total rebellion of God's word.

The Pride of Sodom

Sodom and the surrounding cities were full of pride and homo-sexual lust. A nation that becomes prideful soon is given over to homosexuality and other perversions. Let us read Josephus and see what happened to this proud city:

> About this time the Sodomites grew proud, on account of their riches and great wealth: they became unjust toward men, and impious toward God, insomuch that they did not call to mind the advantages they received from Him: They hated strangers and abused themselves with sod-omitical practices. God was therefore much dis-pleased at them, and determined to punish them for their pride, and to overthrow their city, and to lay waste their country, until there should neither plant nor fruit grow out of it.
>
> When God had thus resolved concerning the Sodomites, Abraham, as he sat by the oak of Mambre, at the door of his tent, saw three angels; and, thinking them to be strangers, he rose up and saluted them, and desired they would accept of an entertainment, and abide with him; to which when they agreed, he ordered cakes of meal to be made presently: and when he had slain a calf, he roasted it, and brought it to them, as they sat under the oak. Now they made a show of eat-

ing; and besides, they asked him about his wife Sarah, where she was; and when he said she was within, they said they would come again hereafter, and find her become a mother. Upon which the woman laughed and said that it was impossible she should bear children, since she was ninety years of age, and her husband was a hundred. Then they concealed themselves no longer but declared that they were angels of God; and that one of them was sent to inform them about the child, and two of the overthrow of Sodom.

When Abraham heard this, he was grieved for the Sodomites; and he rose up, and besought God for them, and entreated Him that He would not destroy the righteous with the wicked. And when God had replied that there was no good man among the Sodomites; for if there were but ten such men among them, He would not punish any of them for their sins, Abraham held his peace.

And the angels came to the city of the Sodomites, and Lot entreated them to accept of a lodging with him; for he was a very generous and hospitable man, and one that had learned to imitate the goodness of Abraham. Now when the Sodomites saw the young men to be of beautiful countenances, and this to an extraordinary degree, and that they took up their lodgings with Lot, they resolved themselves to enjoy these beautiful boys by force and violence; and when Lot exhorted them to sobriety, and not to offer anything immodest to the strangers, but to have regard to their lodging in his house; and promised, that if their inclinations could not be governed, he would expose his daughters to their lust, instead of these strangers—neither thus were they made ashamed.

But God was much displeased at their impudent behavior, so that He both smote those men with blindness and condemned the Sodomites to universal destruction. But Lot, upon God's informing him of the future destruction of the sodomites went away, taking with him his wife and daughters, who were two, and still virgins; for those that were betrothed to them were above the thoughts of going, and deemed that Lot's words were trifling. God then cast a thunderbolt upon the city and set it on fire with its inhabitants; and laid waste the country with the like burning, as I formerly said when I wrote the Jewish war. But Lot's wife continually turning back to view the city as she went from it and being too nicely inquisitive what would become of it although God had forbidden her to do so, was changed into a pillar of salt; for I have seen it, and it remains at this day. (Josephus book 1, chapter XI).

When a nation becomes prosperous, and they forget that it is the Lord who blessed them but instead boasts it of themselves, these perversions rise up because the Lord hands them over to a reprobate mind.

The following scriptures shows what the Lord thinks of these practices:

- "Do not have sexual relations with a man as one does with a woman; that is detestable" (Leviticus 18:22).
- "If a man has sexual relations with a man as one does with a woman, both of them have done what is detestable. They are to be put to death; their blood will be on their own heads" (Leviticus 20:13).
- "Do you not know that wrongdoers will not inherit the kingdom of God? Do not be deceived: Neither the sexually

immoral nor idolaters nor adulterers nor men who have sex with men nor thieves nor the greedy nor drunkards nor slanderers nor swindlers will inherit the kingdom of God" (1 Corinthians 6:9–10).

- "Because of this, God gave them over to shameful lusts. Even their women exchanged natural sexual relations for the unnatural ones. In the same way the men also abandoned natural relations with women and were inflamed with lust for one another. Men committed shameful acts with other men and received in themselves the due penalty for their error" (Romans 1:26–27).

No, there is no such thing as a gay Christian. They are not written in the Lamb's book of life. The Lord does not wink at this sin. He calls it detestable.

Ancient Egypt

After the dispersal, nations began to form around the world. The first major empire was Egypt, and its influence on the world still resonates today. Their worship of the son of the morning was very deep. Pyramids and obelisks were built in honor of their gods.

Ra is the sun deity of ancient Egypt. His image is a man's body with a falcon head. Atop his head is a sun disk enveloped by a serpent. We know the serpent was in the garden, and he is Lucifer. When they worshipped the sun, they were worshipping Lucifer. As the sun was the source of physical light, so the serpent was the source of obtaining the knowledge of good and evil. Along with Ra, they worshipped Osiris, Isis, and Horus, and these gods are still worshipped today as we will see later.

According to Egyptian myth, Osiris, who is the god of the afterlife, the underworld, the dead and resurrection, is the brother of Isis. Osiris was killed by his brother Set and was cut into pieces and his parts dispersed. After finding all his parts except for his penis, which was eaten by a fish, Isis assembled his parts and fashioned a golden phallus (penis) and briefly brought Osiris back to life.

By use of a spell that she learned from her father, she became pregnant by her brother Osiris before he died again. She gave birth to Horus. Since Horus was born after Osiris's resurrection, Horus became thought of as a representation of new beginnings. Osiris is thought to be reincarnated every time the sun rises in the east.

The symbol for Horus is a man's body with the head of a falcon. What is most important is the eye of Horus, which has found its way through the years and is in use today.

Isis is worshipped as the ideal mother and wife and the patron-
ess of nature and magic. Her name means *throne,* and the pharaoh
is the physical representation of her child and so sits on the throne.
The star Sirius is associated with Isis. The star signified the new year,
and Isis is considered the goddess of rebirth and reincarnation. The
model of Isis has made its way through history and has been worshipped with different names in many cultures.

In the second century AD, the Roman writer wrote in his book
The Golden Ass of how the protagonist Lucius prays to Isis as Regina
Calei, "queen of heaven":

> You see me here Lucius, in answer to your
> prayer. I am nature, the universal mother, mis-
> tress of all the elements, primordial child of time.
> Sovereign of all things spiritual, queen of the dead,
> queen of the ocean, queen also of the immortals,
> the single manifestation of all gods and goddesses
> that are, my nod governs the shining heights of
> heaven, the wholesome sea breezes. Though I am
> worshipped in many aspects, known by count-
> less names…the Egyptians who excel in ancient
> learning and worship call me by my true name…
> Queen Isis.

Isis is also shown holding her child-god Horus in her lap. This
would be copied throughout many cultures, finally culminating in
the deifying of Mary holding baby Jesus.

Assyria: Baal, Ashtoreth

The Phoenicians (in the area where the Israelites would eventually settle) worshipped the same gods, just with different names. Baal being the sun god and Ashtoreth (Astarte) the mother-goddess and companion of Baal.

Ashtoreth is the divine mistress and is identified with the planet Venus, the morning and evening star. Being the fertility goddess, wooden poles were erected in her honor representing the male phallus. The obelisk was set in a circle representing the female vulva. Her worshippers would perform sexual orgies before her in hopes of nature imitating them so crops would grow.

> My people ask council from their wooden idols. And their staff informs them. For the spirit of harlotry has caused them to stray, and they have played the harlot against their God. They offer sacrifices on the mountain tops, and burn incense on the hills, under oaks, Poplars and Terebinths, because their shade is good. Therefore, your daughters commit harlotry and your brides commit adultery. (Hosea 4:12–13)

Erecting these things is like sticking it in the face of the Lord God Almighty and saying "Take this, Lord." Total pride and arrogance. Although these sexual orgies aren't practiced in today's society, the objects are still used today. In the center of the Vatican is an Egyptian obelisk sitting inside a circle. This goes back to its roots of paganism when Constantine established the Roman Catholic Church.

Before Protestants point fingers, the high steeple on many churches is a carry-over from Catholicism. Oh, and that Christmas tree and wreath? That is the image of jealousy mentioned in the Bible, the tree being the phallus and the wreath being the womb. Lights are put on to make it hotter and more passionate. Since it represents procreation, it is used for the celebration of the birth of Christ. Most Christians don't realize what they mean, and some don't care because it has been a tradition since they were born, and they just explain it away by saying, "It is now used for good."

The practices before the Ashtoreth poles were an abomination before the Lord and many times in Scripture, He condemned this practice. Let's look at a few:

> Now it came to pass the same night that the Lord said to him, "Take your father's young bull, the second bull of seven years old, and tear down the altar of Baal that your father has, and cut down the wooden image that is beside it; and build an altar to the Lord your God on top of this rock in the proper arrangement, and take the second bull and offer a burnt sacrifice with the wood of the image which you shall cut down.
>
> So, Gideon took ten men from among his servants and did as the Lord said to him. But because he feared his father's household and the men of the city too much to do it by day, he did it by night.
>
> And when the men of the city arose early in the morning, there was the altar of Baal, torn down; and the wooden image that was beside it was cut down, and the second bull was being offered on the altar which had been built. (Judges 6:25–28)

You can see here what God thought about the wooden image. Is anyone brave enough to publicly "cut down" the wooden images of today? Or would we be like our next person who caved to pagan worship so as not to offend?

Solomon was one of the wisest men who ever lived because he started out with a love for God and asked for wisdom. But he had one weakness. His love of many women. He had many wives from pagan peoples, and he became tolerant of their worship of Baal-Ashtoreth and other gods. He allowed this to happen and even participated in it.

> But King Solomon loved many foreign women, as well as the daughter of Pharaoh: women of the Moabites, Ammonites, Edomites, Sidonians and Hittites—from the nations of whom the Lord had said to the children of Israel, "You shall not intermarry with them, nor they with you. Surely they will turn away your hearts after their gods." Solomon clung to these in love. And he had seven hundred wives, princesses, and three hundred concubines, and his wives turned away his heart.
>
> For it was so, when Solomon was old, that his wives turned his heart after other gods: and his heart was not loyal to the Lord his God, as was the heart of his father David. For Solomon went after Ashtoreth the goddess of the Sidonians, and after Milcom the abomination of the Ammonites. Solomon did evil in the sight of the Lord, and did not fully follow the Lord, as did his father David. Then Solomon built a high place for Chemosh the abomination of Moab, on the hill that is east of Jerusalem, and for Molech the abomination of the people of Ammon. And he did likewise for all foreign wives, who burned incense and sacrificed to their gods. (1 Kings 11:1–8)

From this time on, the people of Israel incorporated this abomination with their worship of Yahweh. And today the church has incorporated pagan things into the worship of the Lord.

One of the worst kings to allow this was Ahab, with his wife, Jezebel. She was from a worldly and cultured people and brought four hundred of her prophets of Ashtoreth and four hundred fifty priests of Baal.

> Now Ahab, son of Omri, did evil in the sight of the Lord—more than all who were before him. And it came to pass, as though it had been a trivial thing for him to walk in the sins of Jeroboam, the son of Nebat, that he took as wife Jezebel, the daughter of Ethbaal, king of the Sidonians, and he went and served Baal and worshipped him. Then he set up an altar for Baal in the temple of Baal, which he built in Samaria. And Ahab made a wooden image. Ahab did more to provoke the Lord God of Israel to anger than all the kings of Israel who were before him. (1 Kings 16:30–33)

The Lord had enough and sent Elijah to challenge them. The largest battle took place pitting the false prophets of Baal against Yahweh and Elijah.

> Then it happened, when Ahab saw Elijah, that Ahab said to him, "Is that you, O troubler of Israel?"
>
> And he answered, "I have not troubled Israel, but you and your father's house have, in that you have forsaken the commandments of the Lord and have followed the Baals. Now therefore send and gather all Israel to me on mount Carmel the four hundred fifty prophets of Baal, and the four hundred prophets of Asherah who eat at Jezebel's table."

So, Ahab went for all the children of Israel, and gathered the prophets together on mount Carmel.

And Elijah came to all the people, and said, "How long will you falter between two opinions? If the Lord God, follow Him; but if Baal, follow him." But they answered him not a word.

Then Elijah said to the people, "I alone am left a prophet of the Lord; but Baal's prophets are four hundred fifty men, therefore let them give us two bulls; and let them choose one bull for themselves cut it in pieces, and lay it on the wood, but put no fire under it. Then you call on the name of your gods and I will call on the name of the Lord; and the God who answers by fire, He is God." So, all the people answered and said, "It is well spoken."

Now Elijah said to the prophets of Baal, "Choose one bull for yourselves and prepare it first, for you are many; and call on the name of your god; but put no fire under it."

So, they took the bull which was given them, and they prepared it and called on the name of Baal, from morning till noon, saying, "O Baal hear us!" But there was no voice; no one answered. Then they leaped about the alter which they had made.

And so it was, at noon, that Elijah mocked them and said, "Cry aloud, for he is a god; either he is meditating, or he is busy, or he is on a journey, or perhaps he is sleeping and must be awakened."

So, they cried aloud, and cut themselves, as was their custom, with knives and lances, until the blood gushed out on them. And when mid-day was passed, they prophesied until the time of the offering of the evening sacrifice. But there was no voice; no one answered, no one paid attention.

Then Elijah said to all the people, "Come near to me." So, all the people came near to him and he prepared the altar of the Lord that was broken down, and Elijah took twelve stones, according to the number of tribes of the sons of Jacob, to whom the word of the Lord had come, saying, "Israel shall be your name." Then with the stones he built an Altar in the name of the Lord; and he made a trench around the altar large enough to hold two seahs of seed.

And he put the wood in order, cut the bull in pieces, and laid it on the wood, and said, "Fill four water pots with water, and pour it on the burnt sacrifice and on the wood," Then he said, "Do it a second time," and they did it a second time; and he said, "Do it a third time," and they did it a third time.

So the water ran all around the altar; and he also filled the trench with water, and it came to pass, at the time of the offering of the evening sacrifice, that Elijah the prophet came near and said, "Lord God of Abraham, Isaac and Israel let it be known this day that you are God in Israel and I am your servant, and that I have done all these things at your word, hear me, O lord, hear me that this people may know that you are the Lord God, and that you have turned their hearts back to you again."

Then fire of the Lord fell and consumed the burnt sacrifice, and the wood and the stones and the dust, and it licked up the water that was in the trench.

> Now when all the people saw it, they fell on their faces; and they said, "The Lord, He is God! The Lord, He is God!"
>
> And Elijah said to them, "Seize the prophets of Baal! Do not let one of them escape!" So, they seized them; and Elijah brought them down to the brook Kishon and executed them there. (1 Kings 18:17–40)

This should have changed the hearts of the people to follow the Lord, but the attraction to idols is very strong. When one king would tear down the poles, another would rebel and put them back up again. Here are a couple of examples:

> They set up for themselves sacred pillars and wooden images on every high hill and under every green tree. (2 Kings 17:10)
>
> He removed the high places and broke the sacred pillars, cut down the wooden image and broke in pieces the bronze serpent that Moses had made; for until those days the children of Israel burned incense to it, and called it Nehushatan (2 Kings 18:4)

You see here they even worshipped the bronze serpent. This was made by Moses, so when the people in the wilderness were bit by serpents, they would look toward this pole and be healed. It was a type of Christ on the cross. Those of us bitten by Satan could look to Jesus for healing from sin. Incense in the Bible represents praying. Even today many people worship the image of Christ on the cross, praying to this statue hung on display. Remember, this is something the second commandment said not to do.

Medo-Persia/Greece/Rome

The next major empire to rule was Persia. These were considered an enlightened people because their philosophy was to allow the conquered nations to worship their gods as they like without oppressing them into a national worship. This philosophy continues into the following empires of the Greeks and Romans (although it wasn't until Constantine came to power that Christians were not persecuted for their faith).

When the Greeks came into rule, they were a very worldly people. Many of their games were played in the nude. Nudity was common at banquets. The naked body was considered art, which horrified the devout Jews.

The Greeks also pushed their worship of Zeus upon the Jews feeling that he was the same god as Yahweh. They even wanted the Jews to sacrifice pigs on the altar like they do. This was an abomination.

We can see this in the United States today and around the world. Much paganism has been integrated into Christian beliefs. Also, the worldly culture of the United States has entered into Christian worship services. You can't tell the difference between a rock concert and worship of the Lord.

The Hellenistic Jews who became rich with the Greek culture accepted this mixture in their worship. The others fought to keep the pagan rituals out of the worship of Yahweh. Christians today do the same thing. Many accept the worldly services while the few resist it and are criticized as being legalistic.

When Rome became the world empire, it still retained the Hellenistic culture of the Greeks, worshipping the same pagan gods and considering the emperors and leaders to be gods also. This angered devout Jews because the Syrian empire tried to force these lifestyles on them the century before. The Jewish people knew they were unique because they worshipped one God, and He required them to be separate from the world around them. The devout Jews resisted whenever Roman soldiers entered Jerusalem because the soldiers' standards were poles with insignias on top. This was against the second commandment forbidding "graven images" of any kind. Sadly, even today those Christians who obey God's word and separates themselves are considered fanatical and are shunned and ridiculed. It seems those who are used to pagan symbols being integrated with Christianity because of its long time there don't want to let go. They resist those who speak against it when it is the Holy Spirit leading them to warn that God wants purity and not mixture. If it was an abomination to Him in ancient times, then it is still an abomination today. God is the same today, yesterday, and forever.

The Jews lived with six empires ruling over them over the centuries: Egypt, Assyria, Babylon, Medo-Persia, Greece, and now Rome. They studied the Scriptures looking for the time their messiah would come. They knew from the prophets that the time was near.

> But you, Bethlehem Ephrathah, though you are little among the thousands of Judah, yet out of you shall come forth to me the one to be ruler in Israel, whose goings forth are from old, from everlasting. (Micah 5:2)

> Therefore, the Lord Himself will give you a sign: Behold, the virgin shall conceive and bear a son, and shall call his name Immanuel. (Isaiah 7:14)

That time had come. Gabriel came to Mary to inform her she was chosen to carry Christ.

> Now in the sixth month, the angel Gabriel was sent by God to a city of Galilee named

Nazareth, to a virgin betrothed to a man whose name was Joseph of the house of David. The virgin's name was Mary. And having come in, the angel said to her, "Rejoice, highly favored one, the Lord is with you, blessed are you among women!" But when she saw him, she was troubled at his saying and considered what matter of greeting this was.

Then the Angel said to her, "Do not be afraid, Mary, for you have found favor with God. And behold, you will conceive in your womb and bring forth a son and shall call his name Jesus. He will be great and will be called the Son of the Highest; and the Lord God will give Him the throne of his father David. And He will reign over the house of Jacob forever and of His kingdom there will be no end."

Then Mary said to the angel, "How can this be, since I do not know a man?"

And the angel answered and said to her, "The Holy Spirit will overshadow you; therefore, also that Holy One who is to be born will be called the Son of God. Now indeed Elizabeth your relative has also conceived a son in her old age; and this is now the sixth month for her who was called barren. For with God nothing will be impossible."

Then Mary said, "Behold the maidservant of the Lord! Let it be to me according to your word." And the angel departed from her. (Luke 1:26–38)

Now the birth of Jesus Christ was as follows: After his mother Mary was betrothed to Joseph, before they came together, she was found with child of the Holy Spirit. Then Joseph, her husband, being a just man and not wanting to make her a public example, was minded to put her away secretly. But while he thought of these things, behold, an angel of the Lord appeared to him in a dream, saying, "Joseph, son of David, do not be afraid to take to you Mary your wife, for that which is conceived in her is of the Holy Spirit. And she will bring forth a son, and you shall call His name Jesus, for He will save His people from their sins."

So, all this was done that it might be fulfilled which was spoken by the Lord through the prophet, saying, "Behold the virgin shall we with child, and bear a son, and they shall call his name Immanuel, which is translated, 'God with us.'"

Then Joseph, being aroused from sleep, did as the angel of the Lord commanded him and took to him his wife, and did not know her till she had brought forth her first born son, and he called his name Jesus. Matthew 1:18–25.

I would like to take a moment here and clarify a misconception of who Mary is. Mary never was, nor ever will be, a deity. She is the mother of Christ because she accepted the Lord wanting to use her body to bring Jesus into this world in human form. She could have easily rejected this but didn't. She was a woman soon to marry. There is also a misconception that she is a perpetual virgin even today. This is wrong. You see in this scripture that Joseph "did not know her 'til she had brought forth her *first*-born son." After Jesus was born, they had usual husband/wife relationship and had more children later.

When He (meaning Jesus) had come to his own country, He taught them in their synagogue so that they were astonished and said, "Where did this man get his wisdom and these mighty works? Is this not the carpenter's son? Is not His mother called Mary? And his brothers James, Joseph, Simon and Judas? And his sisters, are they not all with us? Where then did this man get all these things?" (Matthew 13:54–56)

You see here Jesus had brothers and sisters. Mary had many children after Jesus was born.

The following scripture will also show that Mary is not a deity:

> And Mary said, "My soul magnifies the Lord, and my spirit has rejoiced in God my savior. For He has regarded the lowly state of his maid-servant; for behold, henceforth all generations will call me blessed. For He who is mighty has done great things for me, and Holy is His name, and His mercy is on those who fear Him. From generation to generation, He has shown strength in His arm; He has scattered the proud in the imagination of their hearts. He has put down the mighty from their thrones and exalted the lowly. He has filled the hungry with good things, and the rich he has sent away empty. He has helped His servant Israel, in remembrance of his mercy, as He spoke to our fathers, to Abraham and to his seed forever." (Luke 1:46–55)

Mary says, "God my savior." A sinless person nor a deity needs a savior. Mary knew she is a sinner saved by grace and must come under the blood of Christ. She is not interceding for us. She is not to be prayed to. She was born and she died and is awaiting the resurrection as is all who are written in the Lamb's book of life.

"And it is appointed for man to die once, but after this the judgment" (Hebrews 9:27).

Praying to Mary is a type of praying to Isis, the mother-goddess. It is an abomination before God.

Now as to praying to "saints" so they can go before the Father with our petitions, as mentioned before, it is appointed unto man first to die, then the judgment. These who were "canonized" as saints are just people awaiting the resurrection like Mary. The word *saint*

means one who was cleansed and purified by the blood of Christ—
that means all who are cleansed. And long before this canonizing
started, Paul called the people he was writing to saints:

> Through Him we have received grace and
> apostleship for obedience to the faith among all
> nations for his name among whom you also are
> the called of Jesus Christ; to all who are in Rome,
> beloved of God, called to be saints. (Romans
> 1:5–7)

> To the church of God, which is at Corinth,
> to those who sanctified in Christ Jesus, called to
> be saints, with all who are in every place call on
> the name of Jesus Christ our Lord, both theirs
> and ours. (1 Corinthians 1:2)

> To the church of God, which is a Corinth,
> with all the saints who are in all Achaia. (2
> Corinthians 1:1)

> Paul an apostle of Jesus Christ by the will
> of God, to the saints who are in Ephesus, and
> faithful in Christ Jesus. (Ephesians 1:1)

> Paul and Timothy, bondservants of Jesus
> Christ, to all the saints in Christ Jesus who
> are in Philippi, with the bishops and deacons.
> (Philippians 1:1)

> To the saints and faithful brethren in Christ
> who are in Colosse: Grace to you and peace
> from God our Father and the Lord Jesus Christ.
> (Colossians 1:2)

Why would he call them saints if they weren't yet "canonized"? It is because canonizing is a thing of man and not scriptural at all. It is that same mixture of pagan-style worship with the worship of Yahweh, like the Israelites did all those generations.

When the veil in the temple was ripped from top to bottom at the death of Jesus on the cross, God was saying we no longer had to go through a priest to contact God. We now go through Christ for He is our intercessor. If we are under the blood of Christ, then when we stand before the Father, He sees the blood first. That gives us access to Him.

Mystery

Webster's dictionary defines mystery as "something secret." Mystery is mentioned in Revelation when talking about Babylon the Great. In Strong's concordance, it is defined thus: "Musterion—A secret or 'mystery' (through the idea of silence imposed by initiation into religious rites): mystery."

The ancient mysteries as we have seen earlier in this study came from Egypt. It is the worship of the sun god. And we know from Scripture that it is Lucifer who is that sun god. Freemasonry, which is the ancient mystery today, also worships the sun god. And they openly admit it is the same mystery from Egypt. Albert G. Mackey, who was a thirty-third-degree mason and highly respected in the masonic community, said, "The first of which...are those of Isis and Osiris in Egypt. The most important of these mysteries were the Osiric in Egypt." He also said, "Each of the pagan gods had, besides the public and open, a secret worship paid to him to which none were admitted but those who had been selected by preparatory ceremonies called initiation. This secret worship was termed the mysteries."

Manly P. Hall was also a thirty-third-degree mason. He wrote, "In the remote past the gods walked with men and they chose from among the sons of men the wisest and the truest. With these specially ordained and illuminated sons, they left the keys of their great wisdom, which was the knowledge of good and evil. These illuminated ones founded what we know as the ancient mysteries."

Mr. Hall later tells where his wisdom comes from. In his book *The Secret Teachings of All Ages,* he wrote…

> Among nearly all these ancient peoples the serpent was accepted as a symbol of wisdom. Serpent worship in some form has permeated nearly all parts of the earth. The serpent is the symbol and prototype of the universal savior, who redeems the world by giving creation the knowledge of itself and the realization of good and evil. The priests of the mysteries were symbolized as a serpent, sometimes called Hydra. The serpent kings reigned over the earth. It was these serpent kings who founded the mystery schools (post-Babel) which later appeared as the Egyptian and Brahmin mysteries. The serpent was their symbol. They were true sons of light, and from them have descended a long line of adepts and initiates duly tried and proven according to the law.

We know Satan is the serpent. And the serpent is worshipped in the secret societies. But this serpent is also worshipped as the sun. Rev. Alexander Hislop, in his book *Two Babylons,* writes:

> Along with the sun as the great fire god, and in due time, identified with him, was the serpent worshipped. In the mythology of the primitive world, the serpent is universally the symbol of the sun. As the sun was the great enlightener of the physical world, so the serpent was held to have been the great enlightener of the spiritual, by giving mankind the knowledge of good and evil.

As we have seen earlier, only a select few knew who was being worshipped when the ancients worshipped the sun. They had to hide this fact because the general public would object to worshipping

Lucifer. So, they said the sun was a deity and that it had the choice to rise or not. So, the people had to give homage so it would return every day.

Albert Pike, a thirty-third-degree mason wrote:

> The worship of the sun became the basis of all the religions of antiquity. Thousands of years ago, men worshipped the sun. Originally, they looked beyond the orb to the invisible god. They personified him as Brahma, Amun, Osiris, Bel, Adonis, Malkarth, Mithras and Apollo. Krishna is the Hindu sun-god. The Gauls worshipped the sun under the name of Belin or Belinis. The sun is the ancient symbol of the life-giving and generative power of the deity. The sun was his manifestation and because it is the source of light.

He also told who the sun is. "Lucifer, the light bearer! Lucifer son of the morning! Is it he who bears the light? Doubt it not!"

Albert Mackey said:

> Sun worship was the oldest and by far the most prevalent of all the ancient religions. Eusebius says that the Phoenicians and the Egyptians were the first who ascribed divinity to the sun. Hardly any of the symbols of masonry are more important in their signification or more extensive in their application than the sun as the source of material light, it minds the mason of that intellectual light of which he is in constant search, the sun is then presented to us in masonry first as a symbol of light, but then more emphatically as a symbol of sovereign authority.

The use of obelisks was for sun worship. Carl Claudy wrote, "The initiate of old saw in the obelisk the very spirit of the god he worshipped. From the dawn of religion, the pillar, monolith or build up, has played an important part in the worship of the unseen. In Egypt the obelisk stood for the very presence of the sun-god himself."

"The obelisk was consecrated to the sun," said Albert Pike.

Kenneth Mackenzie mentions obelisks also: "Sun worship was plainly connected with the erection of obelisks. They were placed in front of the temples of Egypt."

In masonic rituals, they imitate the sun. They walk around from east to west like the sun.

Claudy explains this ritual:

> When the candidate first circles the lodge room about the altar, he walks step by step with a thousand shades of men who have thus worshipped the most high by humble imitation thus thought of circumambulation is no longer a mere parade but a ceremony of significance, linking all who take part in it with the spiritual aspirations of a dim and distant past. Early man circled altars on which burned the fire which was his god. From east to west by way of the south. Circumambulation became a part of all religious observances.

The reason that they go from east to west by way of the south is referred to in Isaiah 14:13: "I will exalt my throne above the stars of God: I will sit also upon the mount of the congregation in the sides of the north." Lucifer failed to dethrone Yahweh. He hopes to one day change that, so he cannot go into the north.

The masons call that the dark place. Albert Pike said, "To all masons, the north has immediately been the place of darkness, and of the great lights of the lodge none is in the north."

Mr. Hutchens said:

> As in other degrees, the closing ritual provides a summary of the lessons taught in the degrees. We hear in the west the eagles gather and the doom

of tyranny is near, in the south, truth struggles
against error and oppression (the church), in the
north, fanaticism and intolerance wane. (Meaning
worship of Yahweh through Christ and God's
intolerance of sun worship), in the east, the people
begin to know their rights and to be conscious of
their dignity and that the sun's rays will soon smite
the summits of the mountains." He also said, "The
east—the source of light and thus knowledge.

And who is that light? The words of Albert Pike say it directly
on page 321 of his book *Morals and Dogma:* "Lucifer, the light-
bearer! Lucifer, the son of the morning! Is it he who bears the light?
Doubt it not!"

Manly P. Hall wrote, "The master mason is in truth the sun, a
great reflector of light. He stands before the glowing fire light and
the world, through him passes Hydra, the great snake and from its
mouth there pours the light of God. His symbol is the rising sun."
The snake is Lucifer, so when they face the sun, they face Lucifer.

Sadly, sun worship gets into the worship of God's people. He
warned of this in Deuteronomy 17:2–4, 7: "If there be found among
you, man or woman that hath gone and served other gods, and worshipped them, either the sun, or moon, or any of the hosts of heaven,
and it be true that such an abomination is wrought in Israel, so thou
shall put the evil away from among you."

Then the Lord showed Ezekiel the secret things that the elders
were doing:

> And it came to pass in the sixth year, in the
> sixth month, in the fifth day of the month, as
> I sat in mine house, and the elders of Judah sat
> before me, that the hand of the Lord God fell
> there upon me. Then I beheld, and lo a likeness
> as the appearance of fire: from the appearance of
> His loins even downward, as the appearance of
> brightness, as the color of amber.

And He put forth the form of a hand and took me by a lock of mine head; and the spirit lifted me up between the earth and the heaven, and brought me in visions of God to Jerusalem, to the door of the inner gate that looks toward the north, where was the seat of the image of jealousy, which provokes to jealousy.

And behold, the glory of the God of Israel was there, according to the vision that I saw in the plain.

Then said He unto me, son of man, lift up thine eyes now the way toward the north, and behold northward at the gate of the altar this image of jealousy in the entry.

And He said furthermore unto me, son of man, seest thou what they do? Even the great abomination that the house of Israel committeth here, that I should go far off from my sanctuary? But turn thee yet again, and thou shalt see greater abominations.

And He brought me to the door of the court; and when I looked, behold a hole in the wall.

Then said He unto me, son of man, dig now in the wall; and when I had digged in the wall, behold a door. And He said unto me, go in, and behold the wicked abominations that they do here. So, I went in and saw; and behold every form of creeping things, and abominable beasts, and all the idols of the house of Israel, portrayed upon the wall round about, and there stood before them seventy men of the ancients of the house of Israel, and in the midst of them stood Jaazaniah the son of Shaphan, with every man his censer in his hand, and a thick cloud of incense went up.

Then said He unto me, son of man, hast thou seen what the ancients of the house of Israel do in the dark, every man in the chambers of his imagery? For they say, the Lord seeth us not; the Lord hath forsaken the earth.

He said also unto me, turn thee yet again, and thou shalt see greater abominations that they do.

Then He brought me to the door of the gate of the Lord's house which was toward the north; and behold, there sat women weeping for Tammuz.

Then He said unto me, has thou seen this, o son of man? Turn thee yet again, and thou shalt see greater abominations than these.

And He brought me into the inner court of the Lord's house, and behold, at the door of the temple of the Lord, between the porch and the altar, were about five and twenty men, with their backs toward the temple of the Lord, and their faces toward the east; and they worshipped the sun toward the east. (Ezekiel 8:1–16)

The Lord wanted to show Ezekiel what the elders of the people of God were doing in secret. The Lord is also showing us what they are doing even today. He said, "Look at this thing at the inner gate. This image of jealousy was an Asherah pole to the fertility goddess." Today it is the Virgin Mary and even Christmas trees in the front vestibule. This pole was in the gate to the altar. With this abomination, the Lord couldn't even be in the sanctuary. The glory of the Lord departed.

But then He said, "Hold on, there is something even worse." He saw a hole in the wall. This was representative of their minds. So he dug into their minds and saw idolatry and filthy abominations. Today the ministers are obsessed with wealth and the things of this world. They watch things on television and get this filth in their minds and then come and preach to the congregations, all the while having these things imprinted on their minds.

And what is worse is that Jaazaniah, son of Shaphan, stood in their midst. The name Jaazaniah means "heard of Jah." It means to cup your hands over your ears as though you were intently hearing from God. Shaphan means to conceal. So what it is saying is they claim to hear from God and tell you God spoke to them but conceal the fact that they are worshipping the sun god. This is why we have many preachers spreading the doctrine of the word of faith and prosperity gospel and others preaching for decades the gospel of Christ but are in fact a thirty-third-degree mason and secretly worshipping Lucifer, the sun god. This is also why toward the end of a well-known preacher's life, he was compromised and said people of all faiths can enter heaven and not just through the cross of Christ. Satan uses those claiming to be Christ's preachers to deceive multitudes of people with a false gospel so he can bring in a huge harvest to follow him to judgment.

But then the Lord says in verse 13, "it gets even worse." The women were weeping for Tammuz, the fertility god. They were mourning his supposed death at the beginning of summer. They wept for forty days, one day for every year he lived. Today it is called Lent.

Then the Lord said you haven't seen anything yet. Ezekiel looked into the Lord's house at the door of the temple, and the elders had their backs to the temple and facing the east, worshipping Lucifer the sun god. They are doing it today, and the people who call themselves Christian are in the dark about it. But the Lord is letting you know.

We have seen through the ages that Lucifer was worshipped as the sun god so as not to alarm the general public of this fact. It was only known by a few secret groups through the centuries.

Let's now look at the end-time nations that will gather in pride in the final showdown with the Lord Jesus Christ.

The Four Beasts of Daniel

Daniel witnessed five end-time nations who will rise up and prepare the antichrist for the final conflict against the throne of God. Let's look at each beast. I will describe who they are and what role they will play in these end-time events.

When Daniel saw these visions, he had no clue who they represented. He was curious and asked about it. But he was made aware that it was not for his generation but the generation who will be living at that time. That generation would understand the symbols and relate them to whom they represent.

Although I heard I did not understand: then I said, "my lord, what shall be the end of these things?" And he said, "Go your way, Daniel, for the words are closed up and sealed till the time of the end." Daniel 12:8,9.

The Lion with Eagle's Wings

In the first year of Belshazzer, king of Babylon, Daniel had a dream and visions of his head while on his bed. Then he wrote down the dream, telling the main facts. Daniel spoke saying...

> I saw in my vision by night, and behold, the
> four winds of heaven were stirring up the great
> sea, and four great beasts came up from the sea,
> each different from the other.

The first was like a lion and had eagle's wings. I watched till its wings were plucked off; and it was lifted up from the earth and made to stand on two feet like a man, and a man's heart was given to it. (Daniel 7:1–4)

This first beast is England. Her symbol is the lion. It says here the lion walks upright like a man. You can see that in the British coat of arms.

England was key in establishing the way the western nations operate. England once ruled the entire earth. The sun never set on the Union Jack. She is also key in establishing an official language around the world. English is used in everything from air traffic control to many international meetings. It is also a primary or secondary language taught in schools around the world.

England also gave birth to the most powerful nation ever on the earth, the United States. Those are the eagle's wings on her back which are plucked off. This represents the United States becoming an independent nation in a not-so-gentle way. It also has another meaning which we will look at more closely later in this study.

England plays a major role in establishing a foundation for Israel to become a nation. In the book of Haggai, he mentions the date of this event. "Consider now from this day forward, from the twenty fourth day of the ninth month, from the day that the foundation of the Lord's temple was laid—consider it" (Haggai 2:18). The twenty-fourth day of the ninth month on the Hebrew calendar is December 9th on the Gregorian calendar. On December 9, 1917, General Allenby of the English army took over Jerusalem.

It is England who issued the Balfour Declaration, which laid the groundwork for the establishment of Israel. Lord Balfour was a mason, which might explain the six-pointed star of the masons on the flag of Israel.

The Second Beast: the Bear

And suddenly another beast, a second like a bear, it was raised
up on one side, and had three ribs in its mouth between its
teeth and they said thus to it: Arise, devour much flesh!"
—Daniel 7:5.

The bear is the symbol used by Russia. This bear has three ribs
in its teeth. This represents the three major players in the establishment of communism: Karl Marx, Friedrich Engels, and Vladimir
Lenin. It is estimated that around 45 million people were executed
or died in other ways in the Russian Revolution of 1917.

The father of communism, Karl Marx, ironically grew up in
a Christian home. He wrote, "Through love of Christ we turn our
hearts at the same time toward our brethren who are inwardly bound
to us and whom He gave Himself in sacrifice."

Sadly, Karl found Satanism. Through his friend, French socialist
Pierre Proudhon, a satanist, he discovered socialism. Though Marx's
followers are atheist, Karl himself wasn't, for he acknowledged God.
He wrote...

> The abolition of religion as the illusory hap-
> piness of a man is a demand for their real happi-
> ness. I wish to avenge myself against the one who
> rules above. We must war against all prevailing
> ideas of religion, of the state, of country, of patri-
> otism. The Idea of God is the keynote of a per-
> verted civilization. It must be destroyed.

Another "rib" is Vladimir Lenin, a big follower of Marx and
father of the communist revolution. He, too, was Christian who
turned against God after reading Karl Marx's writings. He wrote...

> Atheism is an integral part of Marxism.
> Marxism is materialism. We must combat reli-
> gion. We, of course, say that we don't believe in

God. We do not believe in eternal morality. That is moral that serves the destruction of the old society. Everything is moral which is necessary for the annihilation of the old exploiting social order and for uniting the proletariat. We must combat religion. Down with religion. Long live Atheism. The spread of Atheism is our chief task. Communism abolishes eternal truths. It abolishes all religion and morality. Religion is a kind of spiritual intoxicant, in which the slaves of capital drown their humanity, and blunt their desire for decent human experience. We shall always preach a scientific philosophy. We must fight against the inconsistencies of the Christians.

You see him here attacking Christianity. He said Christianity must be abolished. The old world order must go, and the new world order must come into being.

They aim to convert all who are not atheist. Nikita Khrushchev said, "Do not think that communists had changed their minds about religion. We remain the atheists that we have always been; we are doing as much as we can to liberate those people who are still under the spell of this religious opiate."

China, which adopted communism, killed an estimated 64 million—even higher than Russia. You can be assured that when the United States turns against its people, that number might be much higher.

The Third Beast: Four-Winged Leopard

After this I looked, and there was another, like a leopard,
which had on its back four wings of a bird. The beast
also had four heads, and dominion was given to it.

—Daniel 7:6.

The leopard is the symbol used by Germany. Germany played a major role in preparing things for the last days. Let's look at Germany's history and go over the description of this beast and what it means. There are four heads on this beast. This represents the four reichs. The first Reich was the Holy Roman Empire started under Charlemagne around 800 AD and ending around 1806 AD.

The Second Reich started around 1871 with Otto von Bismarck. Through military skill, he would unify Germany into a great power. This reich would end with the Treaty of Versailles, which ended World War I.

The Third Reich would be the bloodiest. Adolph Hitler's rise to power came through another secret society called the Thule society. It was a part of German Freemasonry, and its prominent member was Dietrich Eckart, the "spiritual founder of Nazism." He was a "dedicated Satanist and the central figure in a powerful and widespread circle of occultists—the Thule society." One person wrote...

> He taught Hitler to worship Satan and use drugs to enlighten his mind and before his death told the people to "Follow Hitler! He will dance, but it is I who have called the tune! I have initiated him into the secret doctrine, opened his mind centers in vision and given him the means to communicate with the powers. Do not mourn for me: I shall have influenced history more than any other German."

Eckart claimed to his fellow adepts in the Thule society that he had personally received a kind of satanic annunciation that he was destined to prepare the vessel of the antichrist, the man inspired by Lucifer to conquer the world and lead the Aryan race to glory.

Hitler chose the symbol of the Luciferian sun god as the symbol of the Nazi party, the swastika.

Rulolph von Sebottendorf, a founder of the Thule society, said, "I intend to commit the Thule society to this combat...I swear it on this swastika, on this sign which for us is sacred, in order that you hear it, o magnificent sun!"

Well, 50 million people died for this evil religion of Lucifer. The symbol for the SS is two lightning bolts in reference to Satan being cast down to earth, as we learned earlier. Germany lost the war but was still influential in establishing a one-world government, as we will see in a moment.

Germany was divided up among the four allied powers of World War II: France, the United Kingdom, Russia, and the United States. These are the four wings on the back of the beast.

Germany would later be a primary nation in establishing the European Union and is the largest contributor. It is the strongest financially out of all the EU nations. (It was given dominion.)

Germany was also a contributing factor in the establishment of the one-world government. A sort of Fourth Reich. After World War I, which was started by Germany, the allied nations formed the League of Nations. This was designed to prevent another world war. This failed, and Germany started World War II along with Japan. After World War II, the allied nations formed what is now the United Nations.

The Fourth Beast

And after this I saw in the night visions, and behold, a
fourth beast, dreadful and terrible, exceedingly strong, it
had huge iron teeth; it was devouring, breaking in pieces,
and trampling the residue with its feet. It was different from
all the beasts that were before it, and it had ten horns.
—Daniel 7:7

The last beast is different than the others because it is not a singular nation but a United Nations, who will unite the world into a singular power to try and conquer God one final time.

The United Nations, though coming into existence in a peaceful way, will and is conquering the entire earth little at a time. It is destroying individual sovereignty of the nations, is dividing up the world into ten bioregions and is acquiring national parks around the world in the name of preservation. This entity will be used by the antichrist and Satan to rule the world. The antichrist will later move his throne from its present position in New York City and establish his throne in Jerusalem where he will rule, making himself as god.

In Strong's concordance, the Greek word for beast is *onpiov.* This means wild animal. But it is also a metaphor for a brutal and bestial man, savage, ferocious. So this man will be a beast, and he will rule the world with an iron fist.

The three other beasts also had a part in the forming of the United Nations as seen in this description:

> Then I stood on the sand of the sea, and I saw a beast rising up out of the sea, having seven heads and ten horns and on his horns ten crowns, and on his heads a blasphemous name.
>
> Now the beast which I saw was like a leopard, his feet were like the feet of a bear, and his mouth like the mouth of a lion. The dragon gave him his power, his throne, and great authority. And I saw one of his heads as if it had been mortally wounded, and his deadly wound was healed. And all the world marveled and followed the beast. (Revelation 13:1–3)

It says here one of its heads was mortally wounded and then healed. The seven heads represent seven world empires over time. Egypt, Assyria, Babylon, Medo-Persia, Greece, and Rome are the previous six. The seventh world power started with the League of Nations. This was designed to prevent another world war. This died when Germany invaded Poland and Japan bombed Pearl Harbor. But it was revived as the United Nations, which was established by the western powers, whose origins are from Europe and the old Roman Empire. And just as the Tower of Babel joined together all people as one to worship Satan as their god, this United Nations is the end-time Tower of Babel designed to do the same. And as the first tower was in the city of Babylon in the land of Shinar, so this latter-day tower sits in the latter-day Babylon (New York City), in the land of Shinar (United States), Babylon the Great.

Deep inside of the United Nations building is a "meditation room." This is to accommodate people of all faiths but nonspecific, bringing all religions together into a single world religion. This room is shaped as a pyramid without the capstone, a trapezoid.

Anton Lavey, who was the founder of the Church of Satan, said that there is a law of the trapezoid. The middle order of the Satanic brotherhood is called "the order of the trapezoid."

Texe Marrs, who was an American writer and radio host, best explains the description of the room:

> The best way to comprehend what the all-seeing eye represents is to examine the architecture of the meditation room of the U.N. building in New York City. The meditation room is… shaped as a pyramid without the capstone. Inside, the room is dimly lit, but coming from the ceiling is a narrow but concentrated pinpoint beam of light which radiates down to a bleak stone altar.
>
> On the wall straight ahead is a modernistic mural that is dynamically endowed with the occult symbolism, containing twenty-seven triangles in various configurations, a mixture of black and white and colored backgrounds, and a snake-like vertical line. At the center is the all-seeing eye which grips the millions of annual visitors with its stark, beckoning image of suspicion.

With the all-seeing eye and the snake, it is obvious that they are worshipping Lucifer, the god of the one-world religion.

> I was considering the horns, and there was another horn, a little one, coming up among

> them, before whom three of the first horns were
> plucked out by the roots, and in this horn were
> eyes like the eyes of a man, and a mouth speaking
> pompous words. (Daniel 7:8)

The word used for *plucked* is *agar*, which means to hamstring. At the time that the United States became an independent nation, there were ten major nations in Europe. Three of those owned territory in the New World and were involved in the war for United States independence. Those nations were England, France, and Spain. All three nations were economically hamstrung and went back to lick their wounds.

The description of this singular horn is important. The word used for *horn* is *qeren*. It means peak of a mountain. If you cut off the top of a mountain, you get a triangle or pyramid. The word also means rays of light. The word used for *eyes* is *ayin*, which means singular eye. So when Daniel was looking at this triangle with a man's eye and rays of light coming from it, he was looking at the great seal of the United States.

The United States became greater than the other countries as stated in Daniel 7:20:

> And the ten horns that were on its head,
> and the other horn which came up, before which
> three fell, namely that horn which had eyes and
> a mouth which spoke pompous words, whose
> appearance was greater than his fellows.

The United States became the greatest superpower in the world, especially after World War II—greater than all the other horns combined.

Before going into more detail about the United States, we will look at what mystery did in Europe before coming to the United States.

Adam Weishaupt is the founder of the Illuminati. He founded it on May 1, 1776. Albert Pike wrote that May 1ˢᵗ was a festival day. "The festival was in honor of the sun."

This secret organization is designed to destroy Christianity, civil government, property, and freedom. The Bavarian government investigated the Illuminati and issued a report: "The express aim of this order was to abolish Christianity and overthrow all civil government."

Adam Weishaupt wrote: "The true purpose of the order was to rule the world. To achieve this it was necessary for the order to destroy all religions, overthrow all government and abolish private property."

To do this, Weishaupt said, "We must do our utmost to procure the advancement of Illuminati into all important civil offices." And they must do it by any means possible. He said, "Behold our secret, if in order to destroy all Christianity, all religion, remember that the end justifies the means, and that the wise ought to take all the means to do good which the wicked take to do evil."

He chose to infiltrate Freemasonry because, from an outward appearance, that organization looked all right to most people. He said, "None is fitter than the three lower degrees of Freemasonry; the public is accustomed to it, expects little from it, and therefore takes little notice of it."

In the three lower degrees, even the participants of masonry themselves are unaware of the true meaning of the symbols and who they represent. It isn't until they advance much higher do they become aware that Lucifer is the sun god they worship. And it is he who wants to destroy Christianity and family.

It is the Illuminati who had influence on the French Revolution. They wanted their own member to be on the throne of France, the Duc O' Orleans. In the 1920s, Nesta Webster wrote about it. "Whilst these events [early stages of the French revolution of 1789] were taking place in Europe, the New World [meaning the United States] had been illuminated."

As early as 1786, a lodge of the order (of the Illuminati) had been started in Virginia, and this was followed by fourteen others in different cities.

Around the same time Nesta Webster wrote that Winston Churchill (who would later become prime minister of England during World War II) wrote in a London newspaper:

> From the days of Spartacus... Weishaupt to those of Carl Marx, to those of Trotsky, Belakun, Rosa Luxembourg and Emma Goldman, this world wide conspiracy for the overthrow of civilization and for the reconstitution of society on the basis of arrested development, of envious malevolence (meaning done with malice, spiteful), and impossible equality, has been steadily growing.
>
> It played a definitely recognizable role in the tragedy of the French revolution. It has been the mainspring of every subversive movement during the nineteenth century, and now at last this band of extraordinary personalities from the underworld of the great cities of Europe and America has gripped the Russian people by the hair of their heads and have become practically the undisputed masters of that enormous empire.

So you see, they influenced the French Revolution, the Russian Revolution, and later on we see how the secret society later influenced Adolph Hitler.

We see here also that it came to the United States concealed in the degrees of Freemasonry so as not to alarm the public.

Adam Weishaupt wanted it concealed. He wrote, "the great strength of our order lies in its concealment; let it never appear in any place in its own name, but always covered by another name, and another occupation."

The Lord knew this would happen, and He revealed it to Zechariah.

> Then I turned and raised my eyes and saw there a flying scroll. And he said to me, "What do you see?" so I answered, "I see a flying scroll. Its length is twenty cubits, and its width is ten cubits." Then he said to me, "this is the curse that goes out over the face of the whole earth: every thief shall be expelled, according to this side of the scroll; and every perjurer shall be expelled according to that side of it. I will send out the curse." Says the Lord of Hosts; it shall enter the house of the thief and the house of the one who swears falsely by my name. It shall remain in the midst of his house and consume it, with its timber and stones."
>
> Then the angel who talked with me came out and said to me, "Lift your eyes now, and see what this is that goes forth." So, I asked, "What is it?" And he said, "It is a basket that is going forth." He also said, "This is their resemblance throughout the earth: here is a lead disk lifted up, and this is a woman sitting inside the basket." Then he said, "This is wickedness!" and he thrust her down into the basket, and he threw the lead cover over the mouth. Then I raised my eyes and looked, and there were two women, coming with the wind in their wings; for they had wings like the wings of a stork, and they lifted up the basket between earth and heaven. So, I said to the angel who talked with me, "Where are they carrying the basket?" And he said to me, "To build a house for it in the land of Shinar, when it is ready, the basket will be set there on its base." (Zechariah 5:1–11)

Zechariah saw a flying scroll. He even gave the measurements, ten cubits by twenty cubits: the measurements of the masonic temple sanctuary.

He said a curse goes out on those who are thieves and perjurers. We already saw that the Illuminati wants to steal people's freedoms and they lie about who they are, who they worship, and what their plans are.

The basket with the lead cover represents the fact that the Illuminati hides their true identity. But the Lord sees all and calls it wickedness. He said you can know this wickedness by their "resemblance." The word used in this passage of Scripture for *resemblance* is the Hebrew word *ayin,* which means singular eye. This is the same eye that Daniel saw.

You notice that the basket is hanging between earth and heaven. This again is the symbol on the great seal of the United States, that unfinished pyramid. This basket is carried by women with wings of a stork. The Hebrew word used is *chaciydah,* which is the feminine form of the word *chaciyo,* which means holy, saint, godly. So they come under the disguise of being holy and godly, saints of the Most High. They even say the eye is the great architect. But an architect can only design from existing materials. He is not a creator. Yahweh creates. Lucifer can only build from existing materials, so they lie about who they worship.

The basket is brought to the land of Shinar. And now we will discuss the land of Shinar.

The Eagle's Wings
on the Lion

Prior to and during the Babylonian captivity of Israel and Judah, the prophets Isaiah, Jeremiah, Ezekiel, Zechariah, Daniel, and Habakkuk prophesied the future of Babylon. But they were not referring to the Babylon of their day. They were talking about the final Babylon in the latter days. "Behold, the hindermost of the nations shall be a wilderness, a dry land and a desert" (Jeremiah 50:12).

The word *hindermost* is *akhareeth,* which means the last or end. Hence, the future (last, latter) end-time, so it is referring to the last Babylon in the latter days.

Jeremiah was looking down through time to the latter days and saw the United States, the youngest major nation. It is the most powerful and prosperous of all nations in history. And this nation will be set up just like Nimrod's Babylon according to Jesus. "And as it was in the days of Noah so it will also be in the days of the Son of man" (Luke 17:26).

Noah lived 350 years after the flood and witnessed his descendant's tower of Babel in the land of Shinar. This end-time Babylon will be a singular nation with a city and a tower where all of the world will come together as one and form a one-world government. It is this land of Shinar that the basket was set down upon.

Manly P. Hall, the thirty-third-degree mason wrote, "Men bound by a secret oath of labor in the cause of world democracy decided that in the American colonies they would plant the roots of a new way of life."

Now, there is no doubt that the Declaration of Independence and the Constitution are the best created documents ever made. No people have had the freedoms that the people of the United States have had. They are losing those rights rapidly through the globalist's ebbing away of freedom. But as you can see in both Scripture and the writings of masons themselves, that mystery came to Shinar through secret societies. And their purpose is to destroy freedom and Christianity.

When the Declaration of Independence and the Constitution were written, the work of democracy was complete. But the designers of the great seal of the United States indicated that the work was not finished as seen in the unfinished pyramid. Members of the Order of the Quest, who designed the great seal, know that their work was not done. They knew that it would take time to undermine democracy and turn people's minds away from salvation in Christ and the blood of Jesus and familiarize them with the ancient mysteries of Egypt.

The eagle was chosen for the symbol of the United States because it was part of the Egyptian symbol for the sun god Ra. Rex Hutchens wrote:

> The eagle…this emblem is of great antiquity figuring in the symbolic inventory of the Egyptians, as the sun, as wisdom is attained through reason, the eagle is also symbolic of reason.
>
> Among the Egyptians the eagle was the emblem of a wise man because his wings bore him above the clouds into the purer atmosphere and nearer to the source of light, and his eyes were not dazzled by that light. Since the eagle also represented the great Egyptian sun-god Anun Ra, it is a symbol of the infinite supreme reason of intelligence.

Kenneth Mackenzie said, "With the Egyptians, the Greeks and the Persians, the eagle was sacred to the sun."

As you can see on the great seal, the eagle with the sunburst above his head is near identical to the image of the Egyptian sun god.

Inside the sunburst is the six-pointed star of the occult made up of thirteen stars.

The all-seeing eye in the triangle above the unfinished pyramid is Osiris, the sun god of Egypt. And as we discussed earlier, the sun god is Lucifer.

Carl Claudy, a mason, wrote, "The all-seeing eye is one of the oldest and most widespread symbols denoting god. The open eye of Egypt represented Osiris."

Albert Pike wrote in his book morals and dogma: "Osiris, the sun, source of light and principle of good." And also, "The all-seeing eye…which to the ancients was the sun."

You remember that thirteen is the number of rebellion in Scripture. It is an important number to the masons also. It is no coincidence that there were thirteen states ratifying the Constitution.

The masons are very proud about the many thirteens on the seal and one-dollar bill. In their magazine *The New Age,* they tell of the fact that there are thirteen leaves on the olive branches, thirteen bars and stripes in the shield, thirteen arrows, thirteen letters in *E Pluribus Unum* on the ribbon, thirteen stars in the green crest above, thirteen stone layers in the pyramid, thirteen letters in *Annuit Coeptis,* and on the front of the bill on the seal is a key, square, and the scales of justice, and a compass which is important to masonry.

But the phrase *Novus Ordo Seclorum* is very important. It refers to the new world order. The secret societies want to abolish the old Christian order and usher in the enlightened new order.

The Eagle's Wings

Now we are going to focus on Babylon the Great. She is an actual nation and not a political or religious system as many believe today. The following will show you that she is a physical nation.

You remember earlier it said in Jerimiah 20:12 that it is the "Lattermost" Babylon he was referring to, and Daniel referred to the eagle's wings on the back of the Lion. Well, Isaiah describes its national symbol.

Woe to the land shadowing with wings, which is beyond the rivers of Ethiopia, which sends ambassadors by sea, even in vessels of reed on the waters, saying, "Go swift messengers to a nation tall and smooth of skin, to a people terrible from their beginning onward, a nation powerful and treading down, whose land the rivers divide" (Isaiah 18:1–2).

The United States is shadowed by the wings of its symbol, the eagle.

Smooth of skin. This is a nation obsessed with removing body hair. They even advertise gadgets on television claiming to remove hair with light. Remember when this was written there wasn't an obsession with this, so it would have been strange to them.

It is a nation that has been feared from its beginning, displacing—sometimes violently—Native Americans from their land and taking over territories once claimed by Spain.

She is treaded down meaning a well-developed infrastructure.

Her land is also divided by the Missouri and Mississippi rivers.

Surrounded by
Many Waters

O you who dwell by many waters, abundant in treasures.
—Jeremiah 51:13a.

The United States is surrounded by many waters. On the East Coast of the mainland is the Atlantic Ocean. On the West Coast, Hawaii and Alaska, is the Pacific Ocean. The Arctic Ocean and Bering Sea are up in Alaska. The Gulf of Mexico in the southern continental US and the Great Lakes in the north.

She is also abundant in treasures. Natural Gas and oil are abundant. She can be energy independent if she wants. She has a lot of material wealth.

Mingled People

A sword against her horses, against her chariots, and against all the mingled people who are in her midst.

—Jeremiah 50:37.

The United States is called the melting pot for a good reason. She is populated by people from all over the earth. She has a large diversity of people.

Then he said to me, "The waters which you saw, where the harlot sits, are peoples, multitudes, nations and tongues" (Revelation 17:15).

There is no other nation in the world with the mixture of national and ethnic backgrounds as in the United States.

The Richest Nation

O you who dwell by many waters, abundant in treasures.
—Jeremiah 51:13a

The fruit that your soul longed for has gone from you, and all
the things which are rich and splendid have gone from you.
—Revelation 18:14.

The United States by far is the richest nation. The standard of
living for most people, including the poor, is better than all the
other countries around the world.

She Has the Number 1 Space Program

Though Babylon were to mount up to heaven, and
though she were to fortify the height of her strength.
—Jeremiah 51:53

NASA is the largest space agency. The United States is well
known for her space program. She has a tremendous star wars
program, has started a space force to coincide with the other armed
forces. She has made it to the moon ("The eagle has landed"), is part-
ner with the International Space Station, and plans to go to Mars.
They are even taking rides into lower space for fun. I'll wait for Jesus
to catch me up to Him, thank you. I'm just saying.

Amber Waves of Grain

Cut the Sower from Babylon and him who
handles the sickle at harvest time.

—Jeremiah 50:16.

The United States is great in agriculture. From the wheat fields in the Midwest to the corn fields of Iowa, potatoes of Idaho, and grapes of the Napa Valley, she is abundant in producing food.

She Has the Number 1 Music Industry

The sound of the harpists, musicians, flutists and
trumpeters shall not be heard in you anymore.
—Revelation 18:22

The music industry in the United States is second to none.
Musicians around the world try to mimic the singers of the
United States because they idolize them. The singer's music has tremendous influence on people around the world. You see children
showing gang signs and signs of the devil and Illuminati at concerts
and on camera because they watch the rappers and singers show the
sign of the devil with their hands indicating who they acknowledge
brought them their fame.

Sadly, much of that type of music has infiltrated into the
churches of Babylon the Great. Worship services look like rock concerts. They want to attract the youth with the worldly style music.
They change to attract them instead of the youth repenting and
changing for Christ.

The United States Does Tremendous Trading

And the merchants of the earth will weep and mourn over her, for no one buys their merchandise anymore. Merchandise of gold and silver, precious stones and pearls, fine linin and purple, silk and scarlet, every kind of citron wood, every kind of object of ivory, every kind of object of precious wood, bronze, iron and marble, and cinnamon and incense, fragrant oil and frankincense, wine and oil, fine flower and wheat, cattle and sheep, houses and chariots, bodies and souls of men. The merchants of these things, who became rich by her, will stand at a distance for fear of her torment, weeping and wailing.
—Revelation 18:11–13,15

The United States is a big consumer nation. Many industries and traders around the world have grown rich from trading with her. Many countries rely on that trading for their economies. The United States has many industries also.

"No craftsman of any craft shall be found in you anymore" (Revelation 18:22).

"And with those industries she has polluted her land. 'Because you have destroyed your land'" (Isaiah 14:20).

She is Proud of Her Advanced Learning Centers

For you have trusted in your wickedness; you have said, "No one sees me," your wisdom and knowledge have warped you, and you have said in your heart, "I am and there is no one else besides me."
—Isaiah 47:10

The United States is well known for her colleges and universities, and it is no secret that these centers of education are godless. In fact, from the time children enter the public school system they are indoctrinated into the belief that they are gods and try to eliminate the belief in the need of a savior.

John Dumphy wrote an essay for the humanist magazine showing this:

> I am convinced that the battle for humankind's future must be waged and won in the public school classrooms by teachers who correctly perceive their role as the new proselytizers of a new faith: a religion of humanity that recognizes and respects the spark of what theologians call divinity in every human being.
>
> These teachers must embody the same selfless dedication as the most rabid fundamentalist

preachers. The classroom must and will become an arena of conflict between the old and the new—the rotting corpse of Christianity, together with all its adjacent evils and misery, and the new faith...resplendent in its promise."

The push to remove the belief in God was written by Paul Blanchard:

I think that the most important factor moving us toward a secular society has been the educational factor. Our schools might not teach Johnny to read properly, but the fact that Johnny is in school until he is sixteen tends to lead toward the elimination of religious superstition.

The average American child now acquires a high school education, and this militates against Adam and Eve and all the myths of alleged history.

In 1963, Madaline Murry O'Hair, being an atheist, successfully removed prayer from school because it offended her. She used her son to report what was going on in school so she could file a complaint in the courts. Fortunately, her son later became a Christian and today is saved. Ms. O'Hair, on the other hand, has found out the error of her ways. She was found murdered and will get to spend eternity floating on the lake of fire she didn't believe in.

The Illuminati has also infiltrated the public school system. Adam Weishaupt wrote:

We must win the common people in every corner. This will be obtained chiefly by means of the schools. We must acquire the direction of education—of church—management of the professorial chair, and the pulpit.

Babylon the Great's schools and universities have become atheistic and humanistic self-deifying institutions, and if you have a different viewpoint than theirs, you are not welcome and are forced off campus.

A Pleasure-seeking Nation

Therefore, hear this now, you who are given to pleasures.
—Isaiah 47:8.

People of the United States love pleasures; whether it be water parks, Disneyland, sports events, fishing, traveling, or any of the many things to amuse them, they look forward to it. They have even spread the pleasures around the world like Disney Japan and Disney Europe. The United States is a pleasure-seeking nation. They schedule their vacation in advance to they can go have some fun.

An Idolatrous People

For it is a land of carved images, and they
are insane with their idols.

—Jeremiah 50:38

Everyone is dull-hearted, without knowledge; every metal
smith is put to shame by the carved image, for his molded
image is falsehood, and there is no breath in them. Therefore,
behold, the days are coming that I will bring judgment on the
carved image of Babylon; her whole land shall be ashamed.

—Jeremiah 51:17–47

Many people of the United States idolize popular people. Whether it be movie stars, athletes, or music singers, they love them. They will use and wear the products the celebrities endorse showing their allegiance. They even have a show that calls them idols. You can't get more blatant than that. They will hang their images on their walls and build carved images and display them for all to see.

But if you look up the images of these stars and politicians, they are making the devil sign, or the 666 sign known as the okay sign showing who rules them.

An idol is that which you put before the Lord God, that which takes a person away from the Lord. When they spend time reading up on the latest celebrity gossip and focus on their lives, they are not focusing on the Lord. And if those celebrities are worshipping Satan, then it is obvious who they belong to.

She is a Nation Full of Filth and Idolatry

And he cried mightily with a loud voice saying, "Babylon the Great is fallen! Is fallen! And has become a dwelling place of demons, a prison for every unclean and hated bird! For her sins have reached to heaven, and God has remembered her iniquities.
—Revelation 18:2, 5

The United States has become a disgustingly filthy place with television shows promoting homosexuality, divorce, and fornication, and people enjoy watching it. Adultery is very common that people aren't ashamed when hearing about it. Homosexuals wanting the right to marry, trampling on the sanctity of marriage. God is removed from public schools, but condoms can be easily obtained with no questions asked.

Disney promoting pedophilia in their images and rides. People seeking readers and advisors instead of seeking the Lord. Many psychics are advertising on television, which was unheard of two decades ago. Churches preaching a weak feel-good message instead of repentance from sin and turning to Jesus and his blood. A pagan obelisk in the capital city of Babylon the Great in defiance of the word of God.

A Violent Nation

Because of bloodshed and the violence of the
land and the city, and all who dwell in it.
—Habakkuk 2:8

The United States has become one of the most violent nations. Gun-related deaths outnumbered all other nations combined in non-warfare killings.

And the new thing today is knocking out unsuspecting people just for the pleasure of it. Children bullying and beating other children. School and mall mass shootings makes it a very violent nation.

Police end up shooting suspects because of the violence they deal with every day, like in the days of Noah.

Cartoons on television and video games promote violence. Children seem to get bored when there isn't any violence in the games.

The Hammer of the Earth

How the hammer of the whole earth has been cut apart and broken.
—Jeremiah 50:23

Because the hammer of the whole earth plundered many nations on its own (Iraq, Afghanistan among others over the decades), she has racked up a huge debt that she cannot possibly pay back.

Then the Lord answered me and said, write in a vision and make it plain on tablets, that he may run who reads it. For the vision is yet for an appointed time; but at the end it will speak, and it will not lie. Though it tarries wait for it; because it will surely come, it will not tarry. Behold, the proud, his soul is not upright in him; but the just shall live by faith.

Indeed, because he transgresses by wine, he is a proud man, and he does not stay at home. Because he enlarges his desire as hell, and he is like death, and cannot be satisfied, he gathers to himself all nations and heaps up for himself all peoples. Will not all these take up a proverb against him, and a taunting riddle against him and say, woe to him who increases what is not his—how long? And to him who loads himself with many pledges? Will not your creditors rise up suddenly? Will they not awaken who oppress you? And you will become their booty. Because you have plundered many nations, all the remnant of the people shall plunder you, because of men's blood and the violence of the land and the city, and of all who dwell in it. (Habakkuk 2:2–8)

In the 1950s, the United States was the largest creditor nation. Today she is the number one debtor nation. With all of her involvement with wars and the violence in the land, she has borrowed trillions of dollars of debt.

A Very Proud Nation

As we just read in Habakkuk, and as I mentioned earlier in the introduction, the United States is a very proud nation. And so blinded by pride are they that they will not repent when reading this writing. But they will puff up even more with prideful anger at reading it, including the proud Christians who are caught up with patriotism more than the humbleness of being a Christian.

> Call together the archers against Babylon all you who bend the bow, encamp around her; let none of them escape, repay her according to her work; according to all she has done, do to her; for she has been proud against the Lord, against the holy one of Israel. "Behold I am against you most proud one." Says the Lord of hosts; For your day has come, the time that I will punish you. The most proud shall stumble and fall. (Jeremiah 50:29, 31–32)

> In the measure that she glorified herself and lived luxuriously, in the same measure give her torment and sorrow, for she says in her heart, "I sit as queen and am no widow, and will see no sorrow." (Revelation 18:7)

> For you shall no longer be called the lady of kingdoms, and you said I will be a lady forever. (Isaiah 47:5, 7)

The United States thinks she is a lady. She has a statue at the mouth of the harbor of Babylon the city to physically show that to the world.

People have bumper stickers saying *Liberty Forever* and *America Forever*. But they don't realize how short her time is. She says she is not a widow, but widowhood will come upon her.

"You say in your heart 'I am' and there is no one else besides me; I shall not sit as a widow, nor shall I know loss of children" (Isaiah 47:8).

"For she says in her heart, 'I sit as queen and am no widow, and will not see sorrow' (Revelation 18:7).

In Isaiah, it tells of Babylon's use of psychics and astrologers to make decisions.

> But these two things shall come to you in a moment, in one day: the loss of children and widowhood. They shall come upon you in their fulness because of the multitude of your sorceries, for the great abundance of your enchantments, stand now with your enchantments and the multitude of your sorceries in which you have labored from your youth—perhaps you will be able to profit, perhaps you will prevail. You are wearied in the multitude of your counsels. Let now the astrologers, the star gazers, and the monthly prognosticators stand up and save you from what shall come upon you. (Isaiah 47:7, 11, 13)

The leaders of the United States have been using astrologers and psychics to make decisions. President Ronald Reagan openly admitted doing this. This is an abomination before the Lord. Yet many people, including Christians, still adore Reagan and said he was a good president and that the United States needs more like him.

But the Lord sees things differently than man. And we have to see things from God's perspective.

Reagan was also given an honorary degree in Freemasonry. Freemasons don't give those unless the person is indoctrinated in the society. This could be why Reagan was the first president to be sworn in facing the obelisk on the opposite side of the White House.

You see here in Isaiah that Babylon has done this from her youth. Even some of the Founding Fathers used psychics for decisions in forming the United States. We already know some worshipped Satan through Freemasonry and the Illuminati, and because they worshipped the same gods as the ancients, the United States is called the daughter of Babylon.

> Come down and sit in the dust, O virgin daughter of Babylon. Sit on the ground without a throne, O Daughter of the Chaldeans. Sit in silence, and go into darkness o daughter of the Chaldeans, for you will no longer be called a lady of kingdoms. (Isaiah 47:1, 5)

> They shall ride on horses, set in array, like a man for the battle, against you, O daughter of Babylon. For thus says the Lord of hosts, the God of Israel, "The daughter of Babylon is like a threshing floor when it is time to thresh her; yet a little while and the time of her harvest will come. (Jeremiah 50:42, 51:33)

She is called the daughter of Babylon because a daughter is just like her mother, in like image. Just like the first Babylon, the United States is the image of her. She is called a virgin because she has never been occupied by a foreign power.

She Will Round Up the Saints for Death

Because the United States claimed to be a Christian nation from the beginning, but also secretly used astrologers and some members were freemasons who learned to worship Lucifer, she is referred to in Scripture as the great harlot. And just like Judas Iscariot claiming to love Jesus but secretly betraying Him, so also will the United States totally turn away from God and betray the true believers in Christ.

Because you were glad, because you rejoiced, you destroyers of my heritage, you have indeed been trapped O Babylon, and you were not aware; you have been found and also caught, because you have contended against the Lord. For she has been proud against the Lord, against the Holy One of Israel. (Jeremiah 50:11, 24, 29)

You will not be joined with them in burial, because you have destroyed your land and slain your people. (Isaiah 14:20)

Let the violence done to me and my flesh be upon Babylon, the inhabitant of Zion will say; and my blood be upon the inhabitants of Chaldea! Jerusalem shall say. As Babylon has caused the slain of Israel to fall, so at Babylon the slain of all the earth shall fall. (Jeremiah 51:35, 49)

I saw the woman, drunk with the blood of the saints and with the blood of the martyrs of Jesus. (Revelation 17:6)

For true and righteous are His judgments, because He has judged the great harlot who corrupted the earth with her fornication; and He has avenged on her the blood of his servants shed by her. (Revelation 19:2)

The United States has already built holding centers around the country for future detainment of Christians and Jews and any others who don't conform to its agenda. They were built for possible terrorists to the United States. But as we can see today, people with a conservative point of view are already considered terrorists. If you try to bring to the people's attention the truth, you are automatically cancelled.

Christianity is hated by those who have been indoctrinated by the elites through secret societies. John F. Kennedy, in a 1961 speech, warned the public that there were those in secret societies in leadership positions who were eager to overstep their bounds and oppress society in the name of national security. He considered it "repugnant." He was silenced in Dallas on November 22, 1963. Interestingly, a member of Skull and Bones was present in Dallas that day. That person later would have a speech of his own stating a new world order. People in leadership positions have gone through the initiations and are determined to establish a new world order and cancel and destroy those in their way.

Most Christian "Leaders" Are Deceiving

My people have been lost sheep; their shepherds have led them astray; they have turned them away on the mountains. They have gone from mountain to hill, they have forgotten their resting place.

—Jeremiah 50:6

We are ashamed because we have heard reproach,
shame has covered our faces, for strangers have come
into the sanctuaries of the Lord's house.

—Jeremiah 51:51.

The shepherds in the churches in the United States have been leading their flocks astray, the word of faith movement being the most prominent, preaching on prosperity saying if you are financially struggling, then you don't have strong faith and you must "sow" the seed into their ministry for the Lord to bless you financially. A pyramid scheme. They are always preaching blessings and good times, always on the mountain, forgetting that it is in the valleys that we are closer to God. Their hearts are not broken because of the sin all around. There is no repentance in their hearts.

They are idolatrous, with a love of money, and a love for the things of this world. I witnessed a shepherd in front of his flock saying he was going to shorten the service because of the big game being televised that day. He jokingly said "If you have sinned, then you are forgiven" while his hand was outstretched toward the congregation.

Then he opened the front of his robe to expose the T-shirt he was wearing underneath with the image of the San Francisco 49ers logo. This was a perfect representation of these people professing faith in Christ on the outside, but inside is idolatry.

Many of these leaders live in extraordinary domains in high society neighborhoods, and when I look at how Christ and the first-century church lived, I see two different churches. They are so out of touch.

And many are teaching that the church will be caught up before the trouble comes. But when confronted with the fact that Christians will be rounded up and exterminated, they say these are the ones who were not ready to go, or they got saved after the Holy Spirit leaves with the Christians. But if it is the Holy Spirit who leads people to salvation, then how do these people get saved? They are teaching something that is not backed up in Scripture. Yes, we will be caught up but not until after the events of Scripture are fulfilled. That is why Jesus said, "He who endures to the end will be rewarded." Paul also said it will be at the last trump. Both Paul and John were in the third heaven. They both knew about the trumpets.

And as for being caught up in the twinkling of an eye, the Bible does not say that. It says we will be changed in the twinkling of an eye. We will probably go up just as Jesus did from His disciples. But I digress.

Babylon Will Not Repent

Many Christians keep praying for the United States to turn around and become godly again. But remember, she has a double life, acting like one nation under God but secretly worshipping Satan and full of filth and idolatry. It also says in Jeremiah 51:9, "We would have healed Babylon, but she is not healed. Forsake her and let us go everyone to his own country; for her judgment reaches to heaven and is lifted up to the skies."

The United States will not turn around. Prophecies will be fulfilled. Better to pray for Christians to wake up and prepare for what is coming.

It says here to flee Babylon. The Lord is telling His people ahead of time to flee from Babylon. Now I don't know for sure if it is physically or just separate yourself from the iniquities of her. If you can leave her, the better. But all nations are turning against God. But definitely separate yourself from the things of Babylon. The following scriptures keep telling His people to flee from Babylon:

- "Up Zion! Escape, you who dwell with the daughter of Babylon." (Zechariah 2:7)
- "Remember, the daughter of Babylon is the latter-day Babylon made in the image of the first Babylon. Go forth from Babylon! Flee from the Chaldeans!" (Isaiah 48:20)
- "Move from the midst of Babylon, go out from the land of the Chaldeans; and be like the rams before the flocks" (Jeramiah 50:8).

- "Everyone shall turn to his own people, and everyone shall flee to his own land" (Jeremiah 50:16).
- "The voice of those who flee and escape from the land of Babylon declares in Zion the vengeance of the Lord our God, the vengeance of his people" (Jeremiah 50:28).
- "Flee from the midst of Babylon, everyone save his life! Do not be cut off in her iniquity, for this is the time of the Lord's vengeance" (Jeremiah 51:6).
- "My people, Go out from the midst of her! And let everyone deliver himself from the fierce anger of the Lord" (Jeremiah 51:45).
- "You who have escaped the sword, get away! Do not stand still! Remember the Lord afar off, and let Jerusalem come to your mind" (Jeremiah 51:50).

Now remember, Jeremiah wasn't referring to the Babylon of his time. They were slaves to Babylon and couldn't flee. He was talking of the hindermost Babylon. We are the New Jerusalem as referenced in Revelation 21:9–22. Those written in the Lamb's book of life are His bride. And we are to keep ourselves pure before him, so as it says, keep Jerusalem in your mind. Stay pure before Him.

John the apostle wrote, "And I heard another voice from heaven saying, 'Come out of her my people, lest you share in her sins, and lest you receive of her plagues'" (Revelation 18:4).

This is obviously the end-time Babylon since at the time John wrote Revelation, Jeremiah's Babylon no longer existed. The Lord always forewarns His people.

"Your mother shall be deeply ashamed; she who bore you shall be ashamed, behold the hindermost of nations shall be a wilderness, a dry land and a desert" (Jeremiah 50:12).

Her mother (England) will be ashamed of her iniquities. Ancient Babylon didn't have a mother. It was started by Nimrod. The United States and England are the only nations to have a mother-daughter relationship.

Again, the hindermost of nations is referring to her being the final major nation in the latter days.

The Great Harlot

This hindermost Babylon is called a harlot because she claims to be a Christian nation but has secretly worshipped Satan through mystery.

"And upon her forehead was a name written, mystery, Babylon the Great, the mother of harlots and abominations of the earth" (Revelation 17:5).

Here in Revelation 17, she wears purple and scarlet. Purple represents following the King of kings who is Christ. But scarlet represents sin and corruption. She has a dual lifestyle.

> Babylon hath been a golden cup in the Lord's hand, that made all the earth drunken. The nations have drunken of her wine; therefore, the nations are mad. (Jeremiah 51:7)

> For all the nations have drunk of the wine of the wrath of her fornication, the kings of the earth have committed fornication with her, and the merchants of the earth have became rich through the abundance of her luxury. (Revelation 18:3)

People of other nations want to be like the United States. They mimic her in everything she does. Whether it be filthy music, shows, or other unclean practices, she has made the world drunk with her iniquity.

As mentioned before, mystery came to Shinar and set up shop. The design of Washington, DC, has freemason fingerprints all over it: a pagan obelisk erected to the sun god, the streets set up in the shape of a goat's head, and an inverted star of the occult.

And as mentioned, the Tower of Babel (United Nations) is set up in the city of Babylon (New York City) in the Land of Shinar (USA). I fail to see how believers in Christ can be proud of that.

She Sits on Seven Mountains

Here is the mind which has wisdom: the seven heads
are seven mountains on which the woman sits.
—Revelation 17:9.

As mentioned earlier, the United States is the greatest superpower and has influence on every continent around the world. The same goes for the United Nations.

It says here she sits on seven mountains. The surface of the earth is made up of mostly seas as a result of the great flood. Out of these seas rise up seven continents. Since the seas are so deep, these continents are mountains penetrating the surface. Since the United States and United Nations have influence over the whole earth, she sits on these seven mountains.

Statue of Liberty

Designed by Frederic Auguste Bartholdi, a mason, the statue is a robed female figure representing the Roman goddess of freedom, Libertas. Bartholdi chose what is now Liberty Island, which was a former army fort. The walls of the fort were shaped as an eleven-pointed star. Perfect, since eleven is an important number in Freemasonry. This wall was used as the base for the statue.

The statue has a broken chain at her feet representing breaking their "bondages of oppression."

> Why do the nations rage, and the people plot a vain thing? The kings of the earth set themselves, and the rulers take counsel together, against the Lord, and against His anointed saying, "Let us break their bonds in pieces and cast away their cords from us." (Psalm 2:1–3)

As we have seen throughout time, man doesn't want the Lord to rule them. They want to be free from his "bondages."

The name of the statue is called "Liberty enlightening the world." This is what the masons and new agers want. They want to "enlighten" the world. Satan has been doing this since the garden, wanting to enlighten the minds of mankind.

President Grover Cleveland said in his dedication speech, "[The statue's] stream of light shall pierce the darkness of ignorance and man's oppression until liberty enlightens the world." That unfinished work of the pyramid is the great seal.

On the head of the statue are the seven rays to form a halo. They evoke the sun, the seven seas, and the seven continents—the seven mountains she sits upon in Revelation 17:9.

The pride of the people of the United States causes many of its citizens to believe that she will live forever. But the Bible clearly states that her end will be soon.

> "Prepare slaughter for his children because of the iniquity of their fathers, lest they rise up and posses the land, and fill the face of the world with cities. For I will rise up against them." Says the Lord of hosts, "and cut off from Babylon the name and remnant, and offspring and posterity," says the Lord. "I will also make it a possession for the porcupine and marshes of muddy water, I will sweep it with the broom of destruction." (Isaiah 14:21–23)

> Because of the wrath of the Lord, she shall not be inhabited, but she shall be wholly desolate. Everyone who goes by Babylon shall be horrified and hiss at all her plagues. Go up against the Land of Merathaim, against it, and against the inhabitants of Pekod. "Waste and utterly destroy them." Says the Lord, "and do according to all that I have commanded you." How Babylon has become a desolation among the nations! The Lord has opened his armory and has brought out the weapons of his indignation, for this is the word of the Lord God of hosts in the land of the Chaldeans. Come against her from the farthest border; open her store houses; cast her up as heaps of ruins, and utterly destroy her, let nothing be left. Slay all her bulls, let them go down to the slaughter, woe to them! For their day has come, the time of their punishment therefore the wild desert beasts shall dwell there. With the jackals and the

ostriches shall dwell there. Be inhabited no more forever, nor shall it be dwelt in from generation to generation. As God overthrew Sodom and Gomorrah and their neighbors, says the Lord. So, no one shall reside there, nor son of man dwell in it. (Jeremiah 50:13, 21, 23, 25–27, 39, 40)

Therefore, thus says the Lord: "Behold, I will plead your case and take vengeance for you. I will dry up her sea and make her spring dry. Babylon shall become a heap, a dwelling place for jackals, an astonishment and a hissing, without an inhabitant. They shall roar together like lions; they shall growl like lion's whelps.

In their excitement I will prepare their feasts; I will make them drunk, that they may rejoice, and sleep a perpetual sleep and not awake." Says the Lord, "I will bring them down like lambs to the slaughter, like rams with male goats.

How Sheshach is taken! O how the praise of the whole earth is seized! How Babylon has become desolate among the nations. The sea has come up over Babylon, she is covered with the multitude of its waves. Her cities are a desolation, a dry land and a wilderness. A land where no one dwells, through which no son of man passes.

I will punish Bel in Babylon, and I will bring out of his mouth what he has swallowed, and the nations shall not stream to him anymore. Yes, the wall of Babylon shall fall." (Jeremiah 51:36–44)

And how will she be destroyed? With nuclear fire!

At the noise of the taking of Babylon the earth trembles and the cry is heard among the nations. (Jeremiah 50:46)

Then I continued to watch because of the boastful words the horn was speaking. I kept looking until the beast was slain, and its body destroyed and thrown into the blazing fire. (Daniel 7:11)

And desolation shall come upon you suddenly, which you shall not know. Behold, they shall be a stubble, the fire shall burn them; they shall not deliver themselves from the power of the flame; it shall not be a coal to be warmed by, nor a fire to sit before! (Isaiah 47:11, 14)

For her judgment reaches to heaven and is lifted up to the skies. "Behold, I am against you O destroying mountain, who destroys all the earth says the Lord, and I will stretch out my hand against you, roll down from the rocks, and make you a burnt mountain. They shall not take from you a stone for a corner nor a stone for a foundation. But you shall be desolate forever," says the Lord.

The sound of a cry comes from Babylon, and great destruction from the land of the Chaldeans. Thus says the Lord of hosts: "The broad walls of Babylon shall be utterly broken, and her high gates shall be burned with fire; the people will labor in vain, and the nations, because of the fire, and they shall be weary.

Now it shall be when you have finished reading this book, that you shall tie a stone to it and throw it out into the Euphrates, then you shall say, thus Babylon shall sink and not rise from the catastrophe that I will bring upon her, and they shall be weary. (Jeremiah 51:9, 25, 26, 54, 58, 63, 64).

Therefore, her plagues will come in one day—death and mourning and famine. And she will be utterly burned with fire, for strong is the Lord God who judges her. When they see the smoke of her burning, standing at a distance for fear of her torment, saying, alas, alas, that great city Babylon, that mighty city! For in one hour your judgment has come. For in one hour such great riches came to nothing. Every shipmaster, all who travel by ship, sailors, and as many as grade on the sea, stood at a distance and cried out when they saw the smoke of her burning, saying, what is like this great city! They threw dust on their heads and cried out, weeping and wailing, and saying, alas, alas, that great city, in which all who had ships on the sea became rich by her wealth! For in one hour, she is made desolate. (Revelation 18:8–10, 17–19)

Again, they said Alleluia! Her smoke rises up forever and ever. (Revelation 19:3)

This is a tremendous fire that can be seen from the oceans. Even the captains fear to come near for the fire and radiation emitting from Babylon the Great. They are watching from the seas because Babylon the Great is surrounded by many waters. This also shows that Babylon the Great is a physical nation and not a political system being taught today. But there will be detractors because the love for Babylon is so great that it overrides the love for God.

Who is this tool for this destruction?

For out of the north a nation comes up against her which shall make her land desolate, and no one shall dwell there in.

For behold I will raise and cause and come up against Babylon an assembly of great nations from the north country, and they shall array themselves against her, from there she shall be captured. Their arrows shall be like those of an expert warrior, none shall return in vain. Behold a people shall come from the north, and a great

nation and many kings shall be raised up from
the ends of the earth. (Jeremiah 50:3, 9, 41)

Then the heavens and the earth and all that
is in them shall sing joyously over Babylon, for
the plunderers shall come to her from the north
says the Lord. (Jeremiah 51:48)

When the Bible mentions a nation from any direction, it is
using Israel as a reference point. If you make a straight line directly
north of Israel, you run directly through Moscow. So the kingdom
of the north is Russia. The United States will finally be destroyed
because of her many sins against God and for the killing of his saints.

Heaven Will Rejoice

Notice also how heaven will rejoice over the destruction mentioned in Jeremiah 51:48. John also describes this event: "Rejoice over her O heaven and you holy apostles and prophets, for God has avenged you on her!" (Revelation 18:20)

> After these things I heard a loud voice of a great multitude in heaven, saying, alleluia! Salvation and glory and honor and power belong to the Lord our God! For true and righteous are His judgments, because He has judged the great harlot who corrupted the earth with her fornication; and He has avenged on her the blood of his servants shed by her. Again, they said, Alleluia! Her smoke rises up forever and ever! And the twenty-four elders and the four living creatures fell down and worshipped God who sat on the throne, saying, Amen! Alleluia!
>
> Then a voice came from the throne, saying, praise our God, all you his servants and those who fear him, both small and great! And I heard, as it were, the voice of a great multitude, as the sound of many waters and as the sound of mighty thunderings saying, Alleluia! For the Lord God omnipotent reigns. (Revelation 19:1–6)

Now if heaven will rejoice over her destruction, then why are so many Christians defending the very same nation that God is angry with? It is because they love the material things the United States has to offer and are blinded to the obvious facts that the United States is the great harlot and will receive her judgment. When they are rounded up and exterminated, perhaps then they will realize their beloved country doesn't love them but despises the things of God. Lucifer hates God and everything that is God's. Until the end, he will try to take everything that is God's, and what he can't, he will destroy.

The Bride at the Wedding Supper

> Let us rejoice and be glad and give him glory! For the wedding of the Lamb has come and his bride has made herself ready. Fine linen, bright and clean was given her to wear. Fine linen stands for the righteous acts of the saints.
>
> Then the angel said to me, "Write, blessed are those who are invited to the wedding supper of the Lamb!" and he added, "These are the true words of God." (Revelation 19:7–9)

This is where I see the people of God being caught up to meet Jesus in the air. It could happen just prior to Babylon the Great's destruction. Either way, we will be with the Lord.

> Brothers, we do not want you to be ignorant about those who fall asleep, or to grieve like the rest of men, who have no hope. We believe that Jesus died and rose again and so we believe that God will bring with Jesus those who have fallen asleep in him. According to the Lord's own word. We tell you that we who are still alive, who are left till the coming of the Lord, will certainly not precede those who have fallen asleep. For the Lord himself will come down from heaven, with

a loud command, with the voice of the archangel and with the trumpet call of God, and the dead in Christ will rise first. After that, we who are still alive and are left will be caught up together with them in the clouds to meet the Lord in the air. And so, we will be with the Lord forever. Therefore encourage each other with these words. (1 Thessalonians 4: 13–18)

I saw heaven standing open and there before me was a white horse, whose rider is called faithful and true. With justice He judges and makes war. His eyes are like blazing fire, and on His head are many crowns. He has a name written on Him that no one knows but He Himself. He is dressed in a robe dipped in blood, and His name is the Word of God. The armies of heaven were following him, riding on white horses and dressed in fine linen, white and clean. Out of His mouth comes a sharp sword with which to strike down the nations. "He will rule with an iron scepter." He treads the wine press of the fury of the wrath of God almighty. On His robe and on his thigh, He has the name written King of Kings and Lord of Lords.

And I saw an angel standing in the sun who cried in a loud voice to all the birds flying in midair, "Come gather together for the great supper of God, so that you may eat the flesh of kings, generals, and mighty men, of horses and their riders, and the flesh of all people, free and slave, small and great."

Then I saw the beast and the kings of the earth, and their armies gathered together to make war against the rider on the horse and his army. But the beast was captured and with him the false prophet who had performed miraculous signs on his behalf, with these signs he had deluded those who had received the mark of the beast and worshipped his image. The two of them were thrown alive into the fiery lake of burning sulfur. The rest of them were killed with the sword that came out of the mouth of the rider on the horse, and all the birds gorged themselves on their flesh. (Revelation 19:11–21)

And I saw an angel coming down out of heaven, having a key to the abyss and holding in his hand a great chain. He seized the dragon that ancient serpent, who is the devil, or Satan, and bound him for a thousand years. He threw him into the abyss, and locked and sealed it over him, to keep him from deceiving the nations anymore until the thousand years were ended. After that, he must be set free for a short time.

I saw thrones which were seated those who had been given authority to judge. And I saw the souls of those who had been beheaded because of their testimony for Jesus and because of the Word of God. They had not worshipped the beast or his image and had not received his mark on their foreheads or their hands. They came to life and reigned with Christ a thousand years. The rest of the dead did not come to life until the thousand years were ended. This is the first resurrection. Blessed and holy are those who have part in the first resurrection. The second death has no power over them, but they will be priests of God and of Christ and will reign with Him for a thousand years. (Revelation 20:1–6)

> The other beasts had been stripped of their authority but were allowed to live for a period of time. (Daniel 7:12)

> These other beasts will still be around for the thousand-year reign of Jesus Christ. The Lion, The bear and the leopard.
> When the thousand years is over, Satan will be released from his prison and will go out to deceive the nations in the four corners of the earth—Gog and Magog—to gather them for battle. In number they are like the sands of the seashore, they marched across the breadth of the earth and surrounded the camp of God's people, the city He loves. But fire came down from heaven and devoured them. And the devil, who deceived them, was thrown into the lake of burning sulfur, where the beast and the false prophet had been thrown. They will be tormented day and night forever and ever. (Revelation 20:7–10)

We see here that people will be living in peace under the rule of Jesus Christ. For a thousand years, they will procreate and multiply on the earth. It is amazing that although they live peacefully for a millennium, when Satan is released, their pride rises and they throw it all away to war with God.

> Then I saw a great white throne and Him who was seated on it. Earth and sky fled from His presence, and there was no place for them. And I saw the dead, great and small, standing before the throne, and books were opened. Another book was opened, which is the book of life. The dead were judged according to what he had done. Then death and hades were thrown into the lake of fire. The lake of fire is the second death. If any-

one's name was not found written in the book of life he was thrown into the lake of fire. Revelation 20:11–15.

So now we know what pride is, and we know what the outcome is. You have a decision to make. Will you humble yourself before God or puff up in pride and tell Him what you think is right? It's your choice. My prayer is that you choose to repent of your sin and turn your life over to Jesus Christ.

About the Author

David Jensen was born in Brick, New Jersey, in 1963. After serving in the US Navy, he settled in South Carolina. After twenty years, he moved to San Antonio, which he has made his home, along with Rowena, his wife, and two sons, Narci and Noah, and mother-in-law, Rosita. David is the author of the book *What Is the New Jerusalem?*, a book about the true meaning of the city of New Jerusalem. He has not always accepted the meaning of the teachings of the church, especially when it comes to prophecy. Descriptions of symbols that weren't understood centuries ago because they weren't for their time cannot be used today because it is our time. He wants to give a better understanding of prophecy so people can feel comfortable with it and not afraid.

9 781685 178420